Language, Poetry, and Memory

Reflections on National Socialism

Harry H. Kahn Memorial Lectures

(2000-2004)

Edited by

Wolfgang Mieder
and
David Scrase

The Center for Holocaust Studies
at the University of Vermont

Burlington, Vermont
2004

© 2004 by Wolfgang Mieder and David Scrase

ISBN 0-9707237-6-8

Manufactured in the United States of America
by Queen City Printers Inc.
Burlington, Vermont

Harry H. Kahn
(1912-1987)

Contents

Preface

Fifteen years have passed since Prof. Harry Zohn from Brandeis University delivered the inaugural Harry H. Kahn Memorial Lecture in 1990. After the fifth annual Kahn Lecture, Prof. Kahn's daughter Hazel Kahn Keimowitz and Wolfgang Mieder edited the book *The Jewish Experience of European Anti-Semitism: Harry H. Kahn Memorial Lectures* (1990-1994) in 1995 with the help of the Department of German and Russian and the Center for Holocaust Studies at the University of Vermont. At that time we expressed the wish that we might be able to put together a second volume for the next set of five lectures, and we did so in 1999 with the book entitled *Shifting Paradigms in German-Jewish Relations (1750-2000): Harry H. Kahn Memorial Lectures (1995-1999)*. And now, another five years later, Prof. David Scrase, founding Director of The Center for Holocaust Studies at the University of Vermont, and Wolfgang Mieder are in the fortunate position to present the eleventh through fifteenth Harry H. Kahn Memorial Lectures in this new essay volume, going on record that we intend to do the same for the next five lectures. In fact, this five-year cycle of Kahn essays has by now become an established tradition at the University of Vermont.

The same is true, of course, for the actual lectures. Many students, faculty, staff, and greater Burlington community members have attended these significant talks, and there are some individuals who have been present at all fifteen lectures. But a lecture is not a permanent record, and we are thankful that the third group of five speakers has given us permission to publish their significant papers in yet another essay volume. We wish to thank Professors Dagmar C.G. Lorenz, Lisa Kahn, Karin Doerr, and Jack Zipes for making this book possible. Prof. Wolfgang Mieder, one of the editors of this book, presented the eleventh Harry H. Kahn Memorial Lecture when Prof. Dagmar C.G. Lorenz could not travel to Vermont because of a snowstorm. While this was a spur of the moment solution, he felt honored at the time and is pleased to include his lecture in this volume as well.

The first five lectures, included in the book mentioned above, were presented by Professors Harry Zohn, Guy Stern,

Sander L. Gilman, Ruth Klüger, and Henri Paucker. The second volume contains the lectures by Professors Egon Schwarz, Karl S. Guthke, Hans Rudolf Vaget, and Doris L. Bergen as well as the address by Madeleine May Kunin, former Governor of Vermont and U.S. Ambassador to Switzerland. To this august list of colleagues and friends we can now add another distinguished group of scholars who are experts in German-Jewish cultural, historical, and literary connections, with a special interest in the study and teaching of the Holocaust. The three volumes with their fifteen Harry H. Kahn Memorial Lectures clearly contain a fascinating array of studies by major scholars.

As was the case with the two previous essay volumes, we are once again including remarks concerning the life and accomplishments of Prof. Harry H. Kahn made by Prof. Wolfgang Mieder, chairperson of the Department of German and Russian, at the inaugural lecture on April 30, 1990. This biographical sketch of the person being honored and remembered with these lectures provides the backdrop to these memorable annual events. The printed lectures are preceded by Prof. Mieder's introductory remarks providing short biographical notes with comments concerning the scholarly accomplishments of the individual speakers.

We thank members of the Kahn family, the Department of German and Russian, and the Center for Holocaust Studies for making the publication of this third volume of Kahn Lectures possible. Special thanks are due Hope Greenberg and Janet Sobieski for their help in preparing the final manuscript of this book. Together we hope that this volume on *Language, Poetry, and Memory: Reflections on National Socialism* will be received with the same enthusiasm as were the two previous books of lectures presented at the University of Vermont.

Summer 2004   Wolfgang Mieder
                                                     David Scrase

Introduction

At the time of the inauguration of the Harry H. Kahn Memorial Lecture Series on April 30, 1990, at the University of Vermont, members of the Kahn family, friends, students, colleagues, and members of the Burlington community came to pay tribute to the memory of Prof. Harry H. Kahn. The Kahn Lecture is now a treasured annual event. It is especially gratifying that Prof. Kahn's widow Mrs. Irene Kahn, his children and grandchildren as well as other members of the extended Kahn family have made yearly pilgrimages to Vermont to be present at these lectures. In his introductory remarks to each lecture, Prof. Wolfgang Mieder includes a concise biographical sketch of the life and accomplishments of Prof. Harry H. Kahn. The longer version of these laudatory remarks was presented at the inaugural lecture in 1990. They introduced the first essay volume of Kahn Lectures in 1995, they were reprinted in the second volume of Kahn Lectures in 1999, and they are here included in full once again to keep the memory of our colleague and friend Prof. Harry H. Kahn alive:

When Professor Harry Helmuth Kahn arrived in the United States in 1940 from his native Germany, he had left behind a political regime of intolerance and horror. Under the inhuman policies of the Nazis a dignified existence in the small village of Baisingen in the Black Forest where Harry Kahn was born into a devout Jewish family on June 20, 1912, was no longer possible. In 1936 Harry obtained a master's degree in Education at the University of Würzburg and then taught in the public school system. He also served as the District Supervisor of Jewish schools in Northern Württemberg from 1935 until his forced departure from Germany in 1939. He had escaped the concentration camp and certain death literally at the last moment. His emigration odyssey led him first to England, then a year later to New York, where he married Irene Levi, who also had barely escaped Nazi Germany from the small town of Rexingen only a few miles from Baisingen. The Kahns arrived in Burlington, Vermont, in 1944 and began a new life there for themselves and their daughter Hazel. Max was born a few years later in Burlington. The horrors of the evil Third Reich lay behind them, but Vermont and its landscape were reminiscent of the Black Forest mountains and became a beloved new home for Harry until his death on November 29, 1987.

Upon his arrival in Burlington, Harry became the principal of the Ohavi Zedek Synagogue Hebrew School, and in 1948 he started his employment as an instructor of German at the University of Vermont. In 1951 he earned a second master's degree, in German, from Middlebury College. He became assistant professor at the University of Vermont in 1952, received tenure in 1958, advanced to associate professor in 1969, and became full professor of German in 1974. When Harry Kahn retired in June of 1977, he did so as a highly respected, trusted, and admired chairperson of the Department of German and Russian (spring 1973 and 1975-1976). Realizing what suffering had been brought to his family and friends by the Nazi murderers, one cannot help but admire Harry Kahn's commitment to teaching German language and culture to American students for thirty years. This work must have caused him pain and grief, particularly during the first years of his employment at the University of Vermont. Harry's influence on many students toward a better understanding of this incomprehensible period of tyranny, horror, and death is one of the invaluable contributions he made during his long tenure at this university.

Harry Kahn's commitment to excellence in teaching is legendary. He also gave much time to his Jewish students as the director of Hillel beginning in 1948. In 1952 he succeeded in starting an elementary and intermediate Hebrew program and taught these courses almost until his retirement. The commitment to Harry's Hebrew courses, as they became known, remains very strong, and it is indeed comforting to know that Hebrew, and now also sometimes Yiddish, are being taught in a Department of German and Russian. It is one of Harry's legacies to have made this seemingly absurd combination of languages and cultures possible. It is, of course, also a clear indication that Harry Kahn had a vision throughout his life that perhaps an improved humanity is teachable and attainable.

His vast knowledge of Biblical and modern Hebrew, religion, the history of Judaism, the Old Testament, and philosophy led him to teach courses in the Departments of Religion, Philosophy, and History in addition to his Hebrew and German courses. Who today would, in this age of overspecialization, be able to teach courses at the university level in five disciplines? Harry's drive to gain ever more knowledge in this broad array of fields is well documented by the intellectual rigor of his last sabbatical in the spring of 1974. At the age of sixty-two he enrolled at the Hebrew University of Jerusalem and took courses in Modern Hebrew, Old Testament, the History of Jews in Moslem Countries, and the History of Anti-Semitism.

Upon his retirement, Harry Kahn began to distribute his beloved and huge personal library to his many friends. Many of us have on our shelves books that contain an "ex libris" card inscribed with "Harry and Irene Kahn." Among my treasures are Harry's four volumes of Thomas Mann's *Joseph Stories*, in which literally every page is covered with Harry's detailed notes, comments, and reflections. It is well known that Thomas Mann employed the technique of "leitmotifs" in his novels, and Harry Kahn's marginal comments give us a good idea of what his own guiding "leitmotifs" were.

Those "leitmotifs," which Harry repeatedly noted, include such concepts as "education," "knowledge," "reason," "rationality," "intellect," and "wisdom." While these reflect Harry's sincere commitment to teaching and learning, he also noted again and again that out of this must grow a "consciousness" of "sin" and "guilt," which in turn should lead to an increased "maturity," "responsibility," "justice," and "truth." Harry also often underlined the word "dream" in these novels, and by quoting just a few additional nouns that he or Thomas Mann used on these pages, we sense what this dream was: a "life" full of "tradition," "dignity," "compassion," "beauty," and "love." The Biblical maxim of "faith, hope, (and) love" is a fitting epitaph for this great teacher and scholar. It is his exemplary service to the University of Vermont and the Burlington community as well as his insistence on finding "humanity" even in the gravest and darkest times that are the legacy of our former colleague and friend Professor Harry Helmuth Kahn.

"In lingua veritas"
Proverbial Rhetoric in Victor Klemperer's
Diaries of the Nazi Years (1933-1945)

Wolfgang Mieder

Introduction

The eleventh annual Harry H. Kahn Memorial Lecture took place on April 10, 2000. Prof. Dagmar C.G. Lorenz, who was supposed to deliver this lecture, could not leave Chicago to fly to Vermont due to a late snowstorm. As organizer of the Kahn lectures, I volunteered to step in at the spur of the moment, with Prof. Lorenz's lecture being postponed to the following year.

There was no formal introduction of me as I stepped up to the proverbial plate to pinch hit, so to speak. It was a matter of letting close to one hundred people go home without a lecture or to fill in for Prof. Dagmar C.G. Lorenz who had tried everything she could to get to Vermont despite the snow. I simply introduced myself and volunteered to present my lecture on Victor Klemperer who as a Jew survived the Holocaust in Germany.

Most of the people in the audience knew me in any case, but since the essays of this volume will hopefully reach many readers outside of the campus of the University of Vermont and the greater Burlington area, let me offer at least a short biographical sketch as will be the case for the other four authors represented by the written versions of their oral lectures.

I joined the faculty of the University of Vermont after having earned my Ph.D. degree from Michigan State University in 1970. Since 1977 I have been chairperson of the Department of German and Russian. In 1980 I was named University Scholar, and in 1987 I was recognized with the George Kidder Outstanding Faculty Award. In 1990 I was named Vermont Professor of the Year by the Council for Advancement and Support of Education. I also received the Certificate of Merit by the Ameri-

can Association of Teachers of German in 1995 and was honored
in the same year with a Kroepsch-Maurice Award for Excellence
in Teaching. In 1997 I was awarded the Giuseppe Pitrè International Folklore Prize for my book on *The Politics of Proverbs:
From Traditional Wisdom to Proverbial Stereotypes*, and in
2002 I was the recipient of the Pizzagalli Construction Company
Celebration of Excellence Award.

As professor of German and Folklore, I have participated in
numerous national and international conferences. My expertise
in literary and folklore studies also earned me guest professor-
ships at the University of California at Berkeley (1981) and at
the University of Freiburg in Germany (1986). While my scholarship ranges from fairy tales, legends, folk songs, and nursery
rhymes to philological and literary studies, I work above all in
international paremiology, i.e., the study of proverbs. Many of
my publications deal with the use and function of proverbs in literature, the mass media, art, politics, advertising, etc. I am also
the founding editor of *Proverbium: Yearbook of International
Proverb Scholarship* (1984ff.) which is published annually at the
University of Vermont. Among my books written in English are
four volumes of *International Proverb Scholarship: An Annotated Bibliography* (1982- 2001), *Encyclopedia of World Proverbs* (1986), *Tradition and Innovation in Folk Literature* (1987),
American Proverbs: A Study of Texts and Contexts (1989), *A
Dictionary of American Proverbs* (1992, with Stewart Kingsbury
and Kelsie Harder), *Proverbs Are Never Out of Season: Popular
Wisdom in the Modern Age* (1993), *The Proverbial Winston S.
Churchill* (1995, with George B. Bryan), *"A House Divided":
From Biblical Proverb to Lincoln and Beyond* (1998), *Strategies
of Wisdom: Anglo-American and German Proverb Studies*
(2000), *"No Struggle, No Progress": Frederick Douglass and
His Proverbial Rhetoric for Civil Rights* (2001), *"Call a Spade a
Spade": From Classical Phrase to Racial Slur* (2002), and *Prov-
erbs. A Handbook* (2004).

It has also been my honor to serve on the Outside Board of
Advisors of the Center for Holocaust Studies at the University of
Vermont and to be one of the instructors of our summer course
on the Holocaust. While I have published articles on such Jewish
authors as Elazar Benyoëtz, Elias Canetti, Erwin Chargaff, Arthur Feldmann, Joseph Hahn, Karl Kraus, and Felix Pollak, there

is also my book on the Jewish cultural critic Moritz Gottlieb Saphir from nineteenth-century Austria. Together with my colleague Prof. David Scrase, Director of the Center for Holocaust Studies, I have edited the following four books: *The Holocaust: Introductory Essays* (1996), *The Holocaust: Personal Accounts* (2001), *Reflections on the Holocaust. Festschrift for Raul Hilberg* (2001), and *Making a Difference: Rescue and Assistance During the Holocaust. Essays in Honor of Marion Pritchard* (2004). It has also been my honor to edit two volumes with the first ten Harry H. Kahn Memorial Lectures together with Prof. Harry Kahn's daughter Hazel Kahn Keimowitz, namely *The Jewish Experience of European Anti-Semitism* (1995) and *Shifting Paradigms in German-Jewish Relations* (1750-2000) (1999). My scholarly and educational involvement with Holocaust Studies and my role as the organizer of the annual Harry H. Kahn Memorial Lectures continue to be an invaluable personal experience.

Lecture

Scholars of language and culture who study the use and misuse of the German language during the twelve years of the Nazi reign have regarded the philologist and literary scholar Victor Klemperer as a key figure for decades. After all, as early as 1947, Klemperer was the first to publish his now famous book *L[ingua] T[ertii] I[mperii]: Notizbuch eines Philologen* [soon to be published in English as *The Language of the Third Reich: A Philologist's Notebook,* in translation by Martin Brady], which started the still ongoing debate about the role of the German language during the Third Reich.[1] While this book, based on diary entries, is still read with scholarly interest and deep compassion for the Jewish author who escaped the horrors of the Nazi era, a two volume edition of Klemperer's diaries has been published in 1995 under the title *I Will Bear Witness. Diaries 1933-1945.* In much greater detail, these volumes present disturbing images of the Second World War and the Holocaust from a victim's perspective. To a large extent, this is done through linguistic observation and analysis. The philologist Klemperer turns his own contemporary history into a "source of linguistic history" and "this philological interpretation is needed to understand contemporary history as cultural history."[2] However, those who interpret "linguistic history as cultural history and cultural history as linguistic history"[3] in Klemperer's sense will not only study individual elements of Nazi vocabulary, but will include the problematic phraseology of that time into their analysis as well. Naturally, proverbs and proverbial expressions are an important partial aspect of such an analysis, particularly since pre-set linguistic formulas played such an important role in Nazi propaganda from war mongering to the persecution of the Jews.[4]

Victor Klemperer, born on October 5, 1881, in Landsberg as the son of a rabbi, began to write a diary when he was sixteen. Even if he did not make daily entries, he continued writing a regular diary until his death on February 11, 1960 in Dresden. He began to compile the most important aspects of his life and time by assembling a *Vita* out of dozens of diary notebooks. The first part of this *Vita* was published posthumously in 1989 in two volumes under the title *Curriculum vitae. Erinnerungen 1881-1918*. In his introduction, Klemperer muses about his manic obsession with writing a diary in typical openness:

> Those who write a *Vita* [...] are concerned about permanency, and want to stay here longer [...]. The wish to stay here means: The wish to play a role [...]; I studied and have achieved a professorship, a rather modest one at that. That is quite an average achievement, and if I were to use it as a claim for an autobiography, it would be bound to be ignored. [...]. Certainly, I have often argued that the average has a special right to receive attention, since it is the fate of the majority to be average.[5]

Of course, Victor Klemperer was far more than an average person. This is evident from four more volumes of diaries now available in print, *Leben sammeln, nicht fragen wozu und warum. Tagebücher 1918-1932* and *So sitze ich denn zwischen allen Stühlen. Tagebücher 1945-1959*,[6] which on several thousand pages present almost 80 years of history experienced and interpreted by Victor Klemperer. It is therefore hardly surprising that the journalist Volker Ullrich entitled his review of the diaries describing life in East Germany with the well-deserved headline "The Chronicler of the Century."[7]

In 1935, Klemperer had lost the professorship bestowed opon him in 1920 at the Technical University of Dresden and then had to spend torturous years of absolute isolation and daily fear for his life in Nazi Germany, courageously assisted by his non-Jewish wife Eva (née Schlemmer) who stood by him as an "Aryan" even after the couple was expelled from their residence in Dölzschen (near Dresden) and forced to live in various "Jewhouses" after 1940. Apart from the forced labor he had to perform in factories, Klemperer had little else to do but manically to give expression to his fate as a former German citizen.[8] As the editor of the diaries Walter Nowojski has noted, the core of the diaries in the period from 1933 to 1945 is a "chronicle of the isolation, incapacitation, harassment, and finally, the systematic annihilation of the Dresden Jews" (II,866).[9] Only the catastrophic air attack on Dresden of February 13, 1945, saved Victor Klemperer from deportation with the last resident Jews and from sure death in a concentration camp. By the death of his companion and fellow sufferer Eva on July 8, 1951, Klemperer had regained a much deserved professorship at Berlin after teaching at Greifswald and Halle universities. In 1952, Klemperer married Hadwig Kirchner (collaborator in the large project of editing the diaries). In 1953, he became a member of the German Academy of Sciences in Berlin. Until his death, he was held in high esteem in East Germany as a victim of National Socialism and as an established scholar.[10]

"I will bear witness, precise witness!" (II,99)

The interpreters of Klemperer's *Diaries of the Nazi Years (1933-1945)* have repeatedly quoted the following characteristic entry of May 27, 1942, which has also found its way into the title of the two volumes of the book *I Will Bear Witness*: "But I continue to write. That is *my* heroism. I will bear witness, precise witness!" (II,99)[11] Nevertheless, it has not been noted that this expression is of course alluding to the proverbial Eighth Commandment: "Thou shalt not bear false witness against your neighbor" (2. Moses 20,16). Klemperer is able to add bitter irony to the Biblical expression "to bear false witness." While the ruling Nazis repeatedly bear false witness against him and all his fellow Jews, he intends to "become the cultural historiographer of the current disaster. To observe until the last, take notes without asking whether the notes will be used" (II,12)[12] by bearing truthful and precise witness. It comes as no surprise that his books *Language of the Third Reich* and *Curriculum vitae* have been praised as "exemplary excerpts of everyday communication in the Third Reich" as well as for their "openness, honesty, and bluntness."[13] With regard to the *Diaries of the Nazi Years (1933-1945)*, critics have spoken of "semantic exposure strategies" and "kaleidoscope stock taking."[14]

Throughout the diaries, "bearing witness" becomes a psycholinguistic leitmotif, as is evident from two more references:

> *June 11, 1942:* I will continue to dare writing the diary. I want to bear witness to the last. (II,124)

> *April 8, 1944*: Conversation with Stühler senior: "I want to bear witness." - "What you are writing is all well known, and you don't know about the big events, Kiev, Minsk etc." - "The big events don't matter. It is the everyday life of tyranny that is forgotten. A thousand mosquito bites are worse than a hit to the head. I observe, I note the mosquito bites ..." (II,503)

Quite obviously, in the latter instance, Klemperer not only uses the "witness" expression, but also adds the proverb "A thousand mosquito bites are worse than a hit to the head," which in the *Deutsche Sprichwörter-Lexikon* (1867-1880) by Karl Friedrich Wilhelm Wander can only be found as the variation "A thousand can do more than one."[15] Klemperer's proverb variant has significantly more metaphorical power and expresses vividly what his main concern for bearing witness is: the normal events of the "everyday life of tyranny." As early as December 10, 1940, Klemperer had come to the same conclusion: "But the changing details of everyday life are precisely what is most important" (I, 565; I,364).

Repeatedly he characterized his work as a tool to fight his fear of death and as a psychological escape mechanism. Thus, he writes on November 29, 1942: "Work, to get intoxicated with work!" (II,285), and on March 15, 1943: "It is difficult to continue working as if I had enough time to complete anything. But working is the best way to forget" (II,344). In a certain way, the absurd Nazi slogan found on several concentration camp gates, "Work makes free,"[16] has been positively true in the case of Victor Klemperer, whose unrelenting will to work and to bear witness about the crimes of the Nazi period fueled his will to survive and gave him the strength to offer valuable services for humanity in spite of the inhuman treatment he received. Martin Walser, in his informative *Laudatio for Victor Klemperer* (1996), correctly speaks of the "professional courage"[17] Klemperer displayed as a scholar and diary writer for twelve years in the face of constant deadly danger. As an outsider and outcast he only had his pen to bear precise witness about human and inhuman behavior during the Nazi period.

"I keep coming back to it: in lingua veritas" (II,75)

On April 25, 1937, Klemperer wrote to his brother-in-law Martin Sußmann in regards to his National Socialist language study "that its motto would be: In lingua veritas" (I, 345; I,216), which precisely defines the base of his socio-psychological language analysis by using a so-called anti-proverb. There are many humorous parodies and innovative alterations of the classical proverb "In vino veritas," but no other instance exists of the very logical phrase "In lingua veritas."[18] Five years later, on April 28, 1942, Klemperer returned to this phrase which completely explains his philological point of view: "But will not my history of language just be a 'disguised' cultural (intellectual) history? No, I have to maintain this: in lingua veritas. Veritas belongs to cultural history; and lingua offers a general confirmation of the facts of interest" (II,75).

Of particular interest in this context is Klemperer's phrase in the *LTI*-book: "Language will bring it to light [i.e., bring out the truth]":

> Whatever someone is trying to hide, be it from others, or from himself, or be it carried around unconsciously: language will bring it to light. That must be the meaning of the phrase: *Le style c'est l'homme*; what a person says may be a lie - but the language style reveals character without fail.[19]

Of course, Klemperer's phrase is a variation of a Grimm fairy-
tale title, "The Clear Sun Brings It to Light" (i.e., Truth will
out).[20] It should be added that Klemperer possibly was familiar
with the ballad-style fairy tale version "The Sun Brings It to
Light" ("Die Sonne bringt es an den Tag") by Adalbert von
Chamisso (1831), where the proverb is repeated at the end of
each of the 14 stanzas as a leitmotif of warning.[21] Actually, "The
sun brings it to light" is also a proverb which is employed by
Klemperer roughly 150 pages later in his *LTI* book as the expressive anti-proverb "Language brings it to light" and is also repeated as a question: "But does language really bring it to
light?"[22]

Klemperer first uses this fitting expression on March 31,
1942, in his diary, and he may have remembered it when he was
preparing the *LTI* manuscript, but he did not take over the exact
quote:

> *LTI*. Language brings it to light. Sometimes, people will
> try to hide the truth by speaking. But language does not
> lie. Sometimes, people will try to give expression to the
> truth. But language will prove truer than they. There is
> no remedy against the truth of language. Medical re-
> searchers can fight a disease as soon as they understand
> its properties. Philologists and poets may recognize the
> properties of language, but they cannot prevent it from
> telling the truth. (II,58)

As a language critic and "judge," Klemperer takes it upon himself to write a "sociolinguistic analysis" of the Nazi years and
"interprets it primarily in a psychological way (language as the
mirror of the damnable actions of human beings; language in the
service of irrationality)."[23] Of course, for the German Jew Klemperer, there is always an element of "being shocked about my
own language" in this analysis. Thus, his entire philological
work turns into a "philology as a defense mechanism,"[24] since
precisely because of his language studies he cannot be reduced to
a powerless victim by his adversaries.

"The shameless shortleggedness of their lies" (II,580)

It should not be overlooked that, in spite of his own intellectual scholarship, Victor Klemperer repeatedly resorted to pro-

verbs and proverbial expressions to get his frustration meta-
phorically speaking "off his chest." This is particularly evident in
his descriptions of the political situation, where he loves to
"play" with proverbs by rephrasing them to characterize the fascist mind set. The following two incidents illustrate the way
Klemperer sometimes accumulates proverbial expressions in his
political musings to "vent his anger" about the steadily deterio-
rating situation. In this context it is interesting to see that in the
first example, he already recognizes the collective guilt of the
German people:

> *October 2, 1938:* I have an expression in my ear that we
> have kept hearing for years now: "We don't know what
> games they are playing." Politics, more than ever, has
> become a secret game of a few who make decisions af-
> fecting millions and claim to represent the people.
> Grammatical despair, subconscious despair. But I quote
> from Bernadin de Saint-Pierre: "If the government is
> corrupt, then the corrupted people are to blame." (I,427;
> text omitted in English version)

> *March 14, 1939:* But now that according to today's eve-
> ning paper the fixed game appears to have been so very
> swiftly and smoothly and completely won by Germany,
> while England and France take it all lying down, I feel as
> sick as a dog again. (I,465; I, 296)

Those are thoughts about world politics in vernacular language
we might not necessarily expect from an intellectual. And yet,
expressions such as "to be a fixed game" or "to take it lying
down" are very well suited to give expression to the whole dilemma. Klemperer's own emotional state lets him resort to proverbial expressions in contrast to his usual abstract style. This
phenomenon was also apparent in the case of the eloquent
Winston Churchill of whom we know that he used his persuasive
and often proverbial linguistic power to fight Hitler's Germany
in verbal and written form.[25]

In a diary entry dated August 17, 1942, Victor Klemperer already notes his thoughts on the German National Socialism and
its organized Holocaust, which much later was scholarly presented by such noted Holocaust researchers as Raul Hilberg.[26] Of

interest is in the following paragraph how Klemperer treats the well-known quotation of the Germans as the "nation of poets and thinkers" (Dichter und Denker) which has its roots in Karl August Musäus' *Physiognomische Reisen* (1779). Karl Kraus' satirical variation "The Germans - the nation of judges and executioners" (Richter und Henker) of 1909[27] seems to have been unknown to Klemperer. This new anti-quotation, which became a popular saying after the disaster of the Hitler-Reich, sadly would have fit the context well:

> National Socialism adapts Fascism, Bolshevism, Americanism, and works it all into a German Romanticism.[28] "Les extrêmes se touchent." Nation of dreamers and pedants, of exaggerated over-consequence, of nebulosity, and of the most accurate organization. Even cruelty and murder are organized for us. Spontaneous antisemitism here is turned into an *Institute for the Jewish Problem*. Nevertheless (les extrêmes), all intellectualism is rejected as Jewish and shallow. Germans feel and have depth. (II,209-210)

Klemperer could have easily used the proverb "Opposites attract," but the Romance scholar and intellectual in this case chose the French equivalent to distinguish himself from the German pedants.

The diaries' main task is to present information about the Nazi state. This is also true in the case of an apparently obvious statement such as the following, where the well-known proverb "Whoever whispers, lies" in a propaganda poster serves to characterize the way Nazi propaganda style is based on fear:

> *June 1st, 1943:* Eva was telling me, that there is a poster all over town - two people whispering- with the caption: "Whoever whispers, lies." And now it occurs to me that they have been writing a long time, a very long time about *whisper propaganda,* and that whisper propaganda is a very characteristic word of LTI and that it must be used in the context of a bad conscience [...]. (II,386)

The mere mention of a proverb abused for the purposes of propaganda is enough to provide the philologist Klemperer with a new idea for his *LTI* research. All this is happening at a time when such actions became increasingly risky for Jews.

Particularly impressive is Klemperer's use of the proverb "Lies have short legs" of September 10, 1944, in order to point out the insincerity of the German regime and its impending downfall: "A special characteristic of the LTI is the shameless shortleggedness of their lies. They forever coolly deny any claims that were made the day before" (II,580). Apparently, Klemperer liked this re-phrasing of the old proverb, and in his *LTI* book we read two years later: "What astonished me was the shameless shortleggedness of their lies, which became apparent in the numbers: The foundation of the Nazi doctrine includes the conviction that the masses are thoughtless and easy to stupefy."[29]

However, what Klemperer writes down on December 14, 1944, as a proverb riddle involving the most popular German proverb "Morning hour has gold in its mouth" seems to prove that the masses couldn't be completely fooled after all: "A new joke riddle is going around, Neumark's secretary, Mrs. Jährig, told us: What is that? It has silver in its hair, gold in its mouth, and lead in its limbs. Answer: The 'Volkssturm' [the forced drafting of all capable males in 1944 to protect Germany resulting in a so-called 'people's army']" (II,627). In this joke riddle, the original proverb is combined with the popular expanded variant "Morning hour has gold in its mouth and lead in its legs (limbs, butt)."[30]

On April 7, 1945, as a refugee in Bavaria, Klemperer tells of another liberating and humorous proverb use in a bomb shelter, where the proverb "Speech is silver, silence is golden" is reduced, half seriously, half jokingly, to its second half - better safe than sorry:

> Conversation with someone there: "How will this war ever end?" The grinning answer: "I can't tell you - silence is golden - you never know whom you're talking to." (II,728)

And how conclusive is Klemperer's statement of May 1, 1945, where the following scene in an inn a week before the end of the war already shows how the majority of Germans will deny that they share any guilt in the Nazi regime:

The innkeeper was loquacious, he told us [...] that he had
never been a member of the Party and how he had wran-
gled with the SA and claimed their respect. How far will
the sails be trimmed to the wind, how far can one trust?
Now, everyone has been an enemy of the Party. If only
they had *always* been... (II,761).

Of course, "the feeling of having been saved dominates"
(II,761), but from the point of view of Klemperer and all other
victims of Nazi terror, the old expression "to trim one's sails to
the wind" is understood as a clear sign of consent, if not of active
participation. Shortly before the end of the war, as can be expected, a lot of opportunists' sails are being trimmed to the wind,
and excuses are available all too readily. On May 5, 1945,
Klemperer notes with distress: "Everything now comes to light
triumphantly that had been most fearfully hidden before April 28
[U.S. troops liberate the concentration camp at Dachau] [...]; no
one wants to have been a Nazi among all those who doubtlessly
played a part. - Where is the truth, how can it even be approxi-
mated?" (II,768). What came to the proverbial light of day were
primarily brazen claims of innocence, and the search for the
truth, despite the large scholarly body of literature written about
the war and the Holocaust, is incomplete to this day. Klemperer's accusing question of May 25, 1945, remains valid today:
"Which part of this not-knowing is the truth?" (II,797).

"An eye for an eye, and a tooth for a tooth" (II,470)

Of course, there is no question about the massive guilt of
Adolf Hitler and Joseph Goebbels, and Klemperer denounces
both men on many pages of his diary. Among other remarks, he
gives evidence of their manipulative use of proverbs and proverbial expressions. With distress, Klemperer reacts on March 31,
1933, to the general boycott against shops in Jewish ownership
proclaimed that day by the Nazi authorities:

Ever more hopeless. The boycott begins tomorrow. Yellow placards, men on guard. Pressure to pay Christian
employees two months salary, to dismiss Jewish ones.
No reply to the impressive letter of the Jews to the
President of the Reich and to the government. - They
murder coldly or "with delay." "Not a hair is harmed on

someone's head" - they only let you starve to death.
(I,16; I, 10, text partially omitted in the English version)

By putting the expression "not to harm a hair on someone's
head" in quotation marks, Klemperer expresses a certain irony.
He is quoting Adolf Hitler, whose "Boycott Call Against the
Jews to all Party Organizations of the NSDAP" of March 28,
1933, was the first official step to exclude Jews from public life
in Germany. Hitler seems to have been convinced that his proc-
lamation was going to cause the Jewish population to leave
Germany:

> The action committees are responsible for ensuring that
> this entire struggle [against the Jews] is carried out with
> utmost calm and discipline. Continue not to harm a sin-
> gle hair on a Jew's head! We will overcome this plague,
> simply by the drastic power of these measures.[31]

Today we know how fast Hitler turned the expression "not to
harm a hair on someone's head" into its opposite by ordering the
physical torture, the murder, and finally the complete annihilation of all Jews. Hitler used the expression with devilish irony, as
he knew in advance that he would go much further than merely
harming the hair of the Jewish citizenry. On August 28, 1933,
Klemperer's diary reports the following malicious joke based on
Hitler's use of the expression. Klemperer and his wife Eva had to
endure the joke when they attended a cabaret show during a
"mystery tour":

> In the cabaret show someone made a joke that nowadays
> seems brazen and could actually cost him his contract. A
> lady wishes to have her hair permed. "Sorry," says the
> hair dresser, "can't do it."- "Why not?" - "You are Jew-
> ish and in Germany, we get punished if we harm a hair
> on a Jew's head." (I,51-52; text omitted in English ver-
> sion)[32]

Such instances are of major socio-political importance and a significant psychological element is added when one considers that
jokes enable populations living under dictatorships to criticize
the system at least indirectly.

On July 20, 1933, Klemperer quotes another expression used by Hitler, which actually characterizes the latter as a paranoid psychopath who hates nothing more than to get laughed at and not to be taken seriously. Those who still laugh literally receive the threat that they will stop doing so sooner or later:

> A sound film recording of Hitler, a few sentences in front of a big meeting - clenched fist, twisted face, wild bawling - "on January 30 [1933; Hitler takes power] they were still laughing at me, they won't be laughing anymore..." It seems that perhaps for the moment he is all-powerful - but the voice and gestures expressed impotent rage. Doubts of his omnipotence? Does one talk incessantly about a thousand years and enemies destroyed, if one is certain of these thousand years and this annihilation? (I,42-43; I, 26)[33]

This is evidence of Klemperer's ability as an insightful psycholinguist with profound understanding of Hitler's psyche. Later, in his *LTI* book, Klemperer returns to this expression and shows how Hitler and his companions turned it from a metaphorical phrase into horrible action:

> One of the frequently repeated and paraphrased Führer phrases is the threat that the Jews would stop laughing, which later evolved into the also frequently repeated statement that they really had stopped laughing. That is true and is confirmed by the bitter Jewish joke that the Jews are the only group for whom Hitler really has kept his word.[34]

Hitler was obsessed with his idea of "Jewish laughter," and kept returning to his threat that those who failed to take him seriously would stop laughing soon. In a speech of November 8, 1942, he claimed that "the National Socialist prophesies are not just phrases," and repeated at the same time:

> If the Jews think they can bring about an international world war to annihilate the European races, the result will not be the annihilation of the European races, but the annihilation of the Jews in Europe.[35] They laughed at me as a prophet. Many of those who laughed back then

are not laughing any more, and many of those who still do may soon stop as well.[36]

The only surprise left here is the word "may" inserted by Hitler, who knew that his own unthinkable murder policy, which ended the lives of millions of innocent people, was already consequently underway.

The otherwise eloquent Klemperer can only respond to Hitler's mendacious politics on December 25, 1941, with a half quoted proverb: "Doesn't he [Hitler] know the proverb: 'Those who lie once ...'?" (I,700). Contrary to the other half of the proverb, "...will not be believed again," millions of Germans continued to believe in the lying demagogue for several more years!

As a last example for Hitler's crazed "populism" it should be mentioned how he blasphemously abused the Biblical proverb "An eye for an eye, and a tooth for a tooth." On January 8, 1944, Klemperer notes as part of his collection of references on the language of National Socialism:

> *LTI.* New Year's Greetings by the leaders. *Hitler:* "Jewish world dictatorship" - "Annihilation of the Jews in Europe" - "with the healthy and fanatical hatred of a race fighting for survival, which, at least in this case, professes to the old Biblical phrase: 'An eye for an eye, a tooth for a tooth'." (II,470)

Hitler had used this Biblical proverb before, in a speech held January 30, 1942. What had been a metaphorical proverb or drastic phrase had now been turned into physical reality. The proverb "An eye for an eye, a tooth for a tooth" (2. Moses 21,24; Matthew 5,38) had been perverted into a popular justification for the actual annihilation of the European Jews:

> We are sure that the war can only end when either the Aryan people have been eliminated or when the Jews disappear from Europe. [...] the result of this war will be the annihilation of the Jews. This time, for the first time, the authentic old Jewish law will be applied: "An eye for an eye, a tooth for a tooth!"[37]

The Holocaust has shown that all of Klemperer's linguistic observations were only too true. This perversion of the ancient proverb of revenge eventually led to genocide, for which there is no proverbial lore.

"The Jewish Question is the A and O" (II,385)

Of course, the linguistic registry of antisemitism is at the core of the *Diaries 1933-1945* and the *LTI* book. In this context, Klemperer mentions the many proverbial placards and headlines, and concludes his entry of September 12, 1937 with: "And the people are so stupid that they believe everything" (I,378; I, 237). Obviously, Klemperer was aware that the National Socialist propaganda machine was subtle enough to base its hate slogans on well-known proverbial structures. This is particularly evident in such antisemitic proverb collections as Julius Schwab's *Rassenpflege im Sprichwort* [Racial Hygiene in the Proverb] (1937) and Ernst Hiemer's *Der Jude im Sprichwort der Völker* [The Jew in International Proverbs] (1942).[38]

Such horrific collections were not known to Klemperer, but some of his diary notes give clear evidence of the proverbial antisemitism of his times:

> *April 25, 1933:* Notice on the Student House (likewise at all the universities): "When the Jew writes in German, he lies," henceforth he is to be allowed to write only in Hebrew. Jewish books must be characterized as "translations."[39] (I,24; I,15)

> *April 17, 1935: Der Stürmer* is displayed at many street corners; there are special bulletin boards, and each one bears a slogan in large letters: "The Jews are our misfortune." Or: "Whoever knows the Jew, knows the devil." Etc. (I,192; I, 118)

> *August 29, 1936:* [Julius] Streicher is speaking in the city today. The preparation for this "major event" has been preceded by all the features of an election campaign: posters, broad banners stretched across streets, processions, drummers and slogans chanted in chorus in the streets. [...] Today the newspaper prints his own words: "Who fights the Jew, wrestles with the devil." I often doubt whether we shall actually survive the Third

Reich. And yet we go on living in the same old way. (I,299-300; I, 186)

May 29, 1943: Stylistically, each sentence, each phrase of the speech [by Prof. Johann von Leer] is essential. The pretended objectivity, the obsession, the popular touch, the common denominator, the emphasis: *The Jewish Question is the A and O.* (II,385)

Repeatedly, Klemperer uses expressions which highlight the increasing antisemitism and the Jewish persecution emphasized by the propaganda:

January 30, 1943: Strange, and impossible to explain to me, how in the government measures, public terror as a prevention measure and secret cruelty go hand in hand. The Jews are hounded mercilessly - but the worst measures against them are kept hidden from the Aryans. Even in close relationships, neither the small cruelties nor the horrible murders are known. (II,324)

February 27, 1943: Note on *LTI:* "Emigrated" for "has been emigrated." Harmless word for "rape," "send away," "send to death." We can be certain now that no Jews will return from Poland alive. They will be killed before the retreat. Besides, word has been that many of those evacuated never even reach Poland alive. It is said that they are gassed in cattle wagons on their way, and then, the wagons stop at a prepared mass grave. (II,335)

These examples make it amply clear that Klemperer in Dresden had full knowledge of the gassing in concentration camps.[40] As early as December 6, 1938, he notes: "The frightful hints and fragmentary stories from Buchenwald - pledge of secrecy, and: no one comes back from there a second time, between ten and twenty people die every day anyway - are awful." (I,443; I, 280). On March 16, 1942, we find the first mention of Auschwitz: "As the worst KZ I heard mention Auschwitz (or some such name) near Königshütte in Upper Silesia. Work in the mines. Death after a few days" (II,47). Then, on January 14, 1943: "The permanent awful fear of Auschwitz" (II,312). And finally, on August 20, 1944, Klemperer writes the following entry, even if he can-

not comment with certainty on the rumor because of his isolation, as is indicated by the attached Italian proverb: "I heard:
Some time ago, a great number of older Jews (three hundred?
three thousand?) had been transported out of Theresienstadt, and
after that, the English broadcast had reported the gassing of the
transport. True? Forse che sí, forse che no" (II,565).[41]

Klemperer's diaries have justifiably been called "steno-
graphs [shorthand notes] from Purgatory," and Klemperer himself has been referred to as a "seismograph of Jewish persecution."[42] The contextualized examples show that proverbs and
proverbial expressions served the cause of antisemitism only too
well, which on the other hand is also a clear indication that these
traditional phraseological units are much more than mere sim-
plistic formulas.

"Vox populi breaks down into voces populi" (I,513; I, 329)

The classical proverb "Vox populi, vox dei" serves Klemperer as a logical leitmotif to characterize his philological observations of the Nazi language.[43] Throughout his notes, Klemperer
wants to record the voice of the people to preserve impressions
of the general atmosphere during the Third Reich. During this
process, he sometimes doubts who and what represents the
"German voice," and whether such a generally applicable voice
even exists. All this, of course, leads to the larger question of the
guilt and responsibility of the German population whose Führer
Hitler understood himself as the "voice of God" for National Socialism. In a speech held March 16, 1936, Hitler already referred
to this originally democratic proverb: "German people [...] I
await your decision, and I know I will be proven right! I will accept your decision as the voice of the people, which is the voice
of God."[44] Of course, Hitler once again only understood this
proverb literally, which is to say, "the voice of the people" for
him only meant the National Socialist German segment of the
population and all other dissenting voices were excluded. Klemperer, on the other hand, speaks in his *LTI*-book of the insolent
lies that were spread by the Nazi leaders under the guise of the
"people's voice" and notes: "However, there is no *vox populi*,
only *voces populi*; and it only can be determined after the fact
which of these different voices is the true one, that is to say,
which of them determines the course of events." A dozen pages

later follows this remark: "*Vox populi* - - always the question of the observer which of the many voices will determine events!"[45] However, the voice prevalent at the time was only that of Hitler himself who claimed the right to be the "*Führer*-God" based on his arrogant interpretation of the entire proverb "Vox populi, vox dei."

Klemperer knows the power held by Hitler and his associates, and their manipulating and propagandistic language is of much concern to him. But the "voice of the people" is of equal interest to him, for "nothing brings us closer to the soul of the people than language."[46] The following four textual examples may serve to show us how Klemperer wrestles with a correct view of the popular voice:[47]

> *September 29, 1939:* Vogel, the grocer: "I don't believe it will last three years, the English will give in, or they will be destroyed. *Vox populi communis opinio.* It has proved in the right with the Russian alliance and the partition of Poland, it could prove in the right now too. There is absolute confidence and intoxication in victory everywhere here. There seems to be no war at all any more. (I,493; I, 314)

> *March 17, 1940:* Rumors and mood change from day to day, from person to person. Whom do I see, to whom do I listen? Natscheff, Berger the grocer; the cigar dealer in Chemnitzer Straße, who is a freemason, the charwoman, whose forty-year old son is stationed in the West and who is on leave just now, the coal heavers. *Vox populi* breaks down into *voces populi*. (I,513; I, 329)

> *January 15, 1944:* Always the same question: Which is the true *communis opinio*, which is the true *vox populi*, the true, determining voice affecting the people and the Army? Nobody knows. The decision comes from some impulse, some group, some prevalent mood; the decision comes from what can be called God, chance, fate, x, - not from consciously leading people. (II,473)

> *February 7, 1944: Voces populi*: On the way to Katz, an older man in passing: "Judas!" In the hallway at the

health insurance company. I am the only star bearer
walking up and down in front of an occupied bench. I
hear a worker say: "A [terminal] injection they should
give them. Then, they'd be gone!" Does he mean me?
The starred one? A few minutes later the man is called
in,[...] I take his place. An older lady next to me, whispers: "That was mean! Maybe he'll have the same thing
happen to him one day that he just wished onto you.
Who knows, the Lord will judge!" (II,483-484)

These ambivalent incidents of the popular voice may serve as
evidence how Klemperer as a reporter not only varies the proverb "Vox populi, vox dei" as a leitmotif, but also how he describes the shifting opinions of the populace. This is enhanced by
the many proverbs and expressions used by the individuals
Klemperer quotes to document their language conventions. The
formulas of popular language are used by antisemites and
philosemites alike to react in a negative or positive manner to
their fellow Jewish citizens. The ambivalent multi-functionality
of proverbial language is particularly apparent here when it is
employed to support opposing arguments.

Klemperer cannot get away from his principal question expressed as a proverb:

May 24, 1941: Always the question: What is the mood
of the people, who can account for it? (I,595; I, 386)

June 22, 1941: What is the mood of the people? Always
my same old question. (I,600; I, 390)

July 19, 1943: The organ play of popular voices. Which
voice will dominate and lead to a decision? (II,406)

As late as February 15, 1945, he speaks with understandable
frustration about the "fickleness of the popular mood" (II,673),
obviously a great problem for someone working as a philological
eyewitness. M.H. Würzner has attempted to interpret this problem of opposing opinions in a short but convincing essay about
"[Klemperer's] Diary as 'Oral History'" (1997): "One aspect
plays a great role in his diary, which is alluded to by the term
'vox populi.' With great frequency, Klemperer notes statements
he hears or are reported to him, and tries to extract from these a

true opinion of the people. [...] What Klemperer notes is 'oral history' in its truest sense. Historians tend to follow the larger outline of the politics of power, but are barely interested in the opinions circulating in everyday life."[48] Terms such as "oral history" or "personal narrative" were unknown during Klemperer's time, but his own proverbial variation "Vox populi communis opinio" (I,493) comes very close to the results yielded by this type of social and folklore research, and his main interest is in this general opinion as the voice of the people. It is not at all easy to find a common denominator for this opinion, as was attempted, for example, by Daniel J. Goldhagen in his controversial book *Hitler's Willing Executioners. Ordinary Germans and the Holocaust* (1996).[49] Justifiably, Klemperer describes his research on the "mentality of a national community"[50] as "voces populi" or "the organ play of popular voices," since *one* true "vox populi" does not exist. On January 22, 1939, he notes in this regard: "No one, whether inside or outside, can fathom the true mood of the people - probably, no certainly there is no general true mood, but always only moods of certain groups" (I,459; I, 293). Here, among other things, lies the great value of the Klemperer diaries; they show us that there simply are no easy answers to the complex questions raised by the Nazi dictatorship and the Holocaust.

"It can cost your head" (II,633)

Of the many somatic expressions found in the *Diaries 1933-1945,* the group around the word "head" might well be analyzed in some detail. The use of proverbial expressions such as "to risk one's head," "to cost one's head," "to come into one's head" and "to be a matter of one's head" in the diaries, even without context, point out that the National Socialist state is a matter of life and death for the Jews. This also applies to Klemperer's non-Jewish wife Eva who engages herself for her husband and other Jewish friends:

> *July 1, 1942:* Eva is increasingly occupied with errands. - For Frau Pick she literally risks her head, no, our heads. ("For your manuscripts, too," she counters my admonitions.) (II,150)

The word "literally" underscores the fact that the proverbial expression "to risk one's head" is not just a cliché. The actual danger for Eva to be intercepted on her errands with her husband's manuscripts was much too great.

Even more direct and drastic are three diary entries in which Klemperer uses the expression "to cost one's head" to characterize the difficult and dangerous situation through a very clear metaphor. In this context, the expression loses its metaphorical meaning and shows in the most obvious way the true danger those people lived in who were not welcome to the government for any reason:

> *April 12, 1944:* [after a conversation with the optician Hahn]: I in the end: "But don't tell anyone, or else you don't need to bother making the glasses; it will cost me my head." (II,504)

> *December 23, 1944:* From Stern and Mrs. Stühler I heard the latest jokes. The difference between Japan and the "Volkssturm" [the people's army]: Japan is the land of smiles; the "Volkssturm" is the smile of the country. - "When Heß went, it was ugly [häßlich]; if Ley went, it would be reasonable [leidlich]; if Himmler went, it would be celestial [himmlisch]." - It is probably without value to note such jokes for LTI: who dares to write such things down?[51] It can cost your head. (II,632-633)

> *April 22, 1945:* And always: "But you know that our conversation will cost your head if..." (II,752)

Doubtlessly, there was a great number of jokes circulating under the extreme policies of the Third Reich; and the philologist Victor Klemperer recognized the deep psychological insights hidden in popular jokes.[52]

At the end of this analysis of the somatic "head" expressions in the diaries, a few more examples citing the positive and encouraging expression "to keep one's head [in English better: chin] up" must be mentioned. These are all moments when German fellow citizens showed human compassion for the German Jew Klemperer. In spite of evil perpetrators and the many silent bystanders, there were also some decent people who had enough humanity and courage to help Jews such as Victor Klemperer or to at least give them a friendly word. The following diary entries seem to express a certain type of charity or, more abstract, an ideal of humanity in Lessing's sense.[53] Maybe such people remembered their old school reading of Lessing's *Nathan the Wise* and simply expressed their understanding of tolerance with the expression "to keep one's chin up." After reading these examples, it becomes apparent that the expression is not employed as a mere popular cliché. Rather, it is a popular way of expressing solidarity for one's Jewish fellow citizens which today moves us as evidence of human charity and sincerity, somewhat remindful of Goethe's request: "Noble be man, helpful, and good!" from his poem "The Divine [i.e., in humans]" (1783):

> *April 16, 1943:* They [two helpful workers] were silent and left. Right afterwards, one of them stuck his head back through the half open door and said in a low voice: "Keep your chin up!" I looked at him with big eyes. Then he added: "Those damned pigs - what they are doing to people - in Poland - I am angry about that, too. Chin up, it will not be forever... they cannot go through another winter in Russia - chin up, things will change ..." (II,352)

> *August 24, 1944:* Yesterday afternoon at the train crossing in front of our house, a wild looking worker came right up close to me and said loudly: "Keep your chin up! Those bastards will soon be done with!" - Stühler had a similar thing happen to him. But on the other hand, we have been seeing this type of event every few days for years, and we have also been experiencing the exact opposite every few days for the same number of years. Nothing can be concluded from that, and nothing from the war situation either, as desperate it may be in both East and West for Germany. (II,567)[54]

Certainly, Klemperer is right in saying that not much can be concluded from all these positive and negative statements. They did take place, and if a workman came back under threat of danger to encourage Dr. Klemperer in simple folk language by using the proverbial expression "to keep one's chin up" three times, and if by doing so he managed to express a little bit of solidarity, we are most impressed with this sign of human decency. Heidrun Kämper also refers to this quoted text from April 16, 1943, and speculates that "such harmless humanitarian signals must have had life-saving value for those persecuted under National Socialism."[55] And even the scholar Klemperer resorts to the expression "to keep one's chin up" to continue his own literary and language studies of the Third Reich with his head held high: "To study as if tomorrow were a sure thing! That is the only way to keep my chin up" (II,214).

"To escape with one's [naked] life" (II,235)

For twelve years, the life of Victor Klemperer oscillates between deep pessimism and small hope, and the fear of a violent death accompanies his every step. On January 14, 1943, we read generally and proverbially: "I am subject to the Gestapo, they are not good to eat cherries with [in English better: they are best not to tangle with]" (II,312), and this wisdom expressed with a certain amount of black humor is followed half a page later by the very realistic statement about the "permanent dreadful fear of Auschwitz" (II,312). The main focus of the *Diaries 1933-1945* is necessarily on life and survival, which of course is reflected in the proverbial expressions dealing with "life." The following chronologically arranged references contain the phrases "to pay with one's life," "to escape with one's [naked] life," "to be a matter of life and death," and "to cost one's life," which, even without context, underscore the precarious situation of Victor and Eva Klemperer:

> *April 3, 1933:* I have the impression of a swiftly approaching catastrophe.[...] There will be an explosion - but we may pay for it with our lives, we Jews. [...] I no longer believe in national psychologies. Everything I considered un-German, brutality, injustice, hypocrisy, mass hysteria to the point of intoxication, all of it flourishes here.[56] (I,18; I, 11)

> *May 18, 1942:* The general mood at Seliksohns was depressed. He keeps claiming that we will not escape with our [naked] lives. (II,87)

September 7, 1942: It is a matter of life and death, I wouldn't challenge these people [the Gestapo]. (II,235)

July 19, 1943: When I returned from the cemetery on Sunday afternoon, there was an older gentleman on the boardwalk at Lothringer Strasse - white goatee, around seventy, a retired higher official - who crossed over to meet me. He gave me his hand and said, with a certain formality: "I saw your star and I salute you; I do not approve of the ostracizing of your race, and many others agree with me." I: "Very kind - but you should not talk to me, it could cost my life and get you in prison." - Yes, but he had wanted and needed to say that to me. (II,406)

Thus, their life is always at the proverbial stake and it is astonishing how Klemperer, with the help of his wife, can muster the ever so weak optimism to somehow survive all his troubles. In this process, he seems to move from one unlikely ray of hope to the next, and proverbs and proverbial expressions, in their popular simplicity, help him mentally to deal with his situation and to give him the courage to go on. An interesting example can be found in the following diary entry of November 24, 1936:

I now have the impression that war is unavoidable; every day brings it closer [...]. We have learned patience and were quite without hope and are still only halfway hopeful, but the pitcher has truly been going to the well for a very long time now, and every day with a greater (perhaps desperate?) foolhardiness. (I,322; I, 200)

Here, the medieval proverb "The pitcher goes to the well until it breaks"[57] serves to give metaphorical expression to the hope that the expected war will also mean an end of Hitler's power and his antisemitic persecution. Such frail rays of hope quickly are followed by fatalistic thoughts, such as on October 14, 1940, where the expression "nobody gives a hoot" characterizes the futility of his work:

Day and night (literally) I am dogged by thoughts of death and futility [...]. Only the end [of the war and Hitler] will show how I spent the last part of my life, whether I shall be considered irresponsibly indolent and

unprincipled or tenacious and self-assured or whether
nobody will give a hoot, myself included. This last
statement is 99 percent likely. (I,557; I, 359)

Besides its convincing honesty, this statement is of interest in the
way Klemperer uses the word "literally" to indicate that there is
nothing figurative about an expression such as "day and night,"
as the fear for his life is at every moment overwhelmingly real.

This honest observation of his own emotions and thoughts is
also apparent in Klemperer's report about the week from June 23
to July 1, 1941, which he spent in "cell 89" in prison. Who
would have thought that the intellectual Professor Victor Klemperer would have used three proverbs in that situation to do a
self-critical appraisal of himself. He accuses himself primarily of
having been driven by "hubris" (I,635; I, 411) and having
brought danger not only upon himself but also his wife Eva.
What follows are excerpts of his self-accusing thoughts written
in prison expecting a certain death:

> But if one settles accounts with oneself, forgiveness is
> self-deception. Can the intention, to do better in the fu-
> ture, help me? First of all, it is very questionable whether
> I still have a future (at 60 and in the clutches of the 3.
> Reich), second doing better never wipes out what one
> has done badly before, and third, - I have always told
> myself that the opposite of every proverb is also true (the
> first step is always easiest, you can teach an old dog new
> tricks ...), but one, about the road to hell being paved
> with good intentions is absolutely to the point. (I,635-
> 636; I, 411)

Even though the term "anti-proverb" was unknown to Klemperer, he forms two such phrases in this short paragraph. Of even
larger importance is of course the fact that Klemperer fully ac-
cepts the proverb "The road to hell is paved with good intentions" in regard to his own life. The proverbial lines actually represent an unexpected self-accusation in a very popular style. In
addition, this triple proverbial statement shows how Klemperer
reduced his entire fate and life to popular wisdom rather than at-
tempting to convey abstract explanations and justifications.

Klemperer finally did "escape with his life." In the truest sense of the word, he was "granted" what he had wished on October 9, 1942: "Perhaps I will be able to survive and bear witness" (II,255). Like a Biblical prophet, Victor Klemperer proverbially "bore witness" in his *Diaries 1933-1945*, not a false, but an honest and exact witness to his life and survival during the Third Reich. Thus, his diaries represent the autobiography of one of the many Jewish victims, but they also are a document of their times of the highest value for linguistic and cultural history. Obviously, Klemperer intentionally used popular proverbs and proverbial expressions to add power to his observations and statements. The proverbial language he shows us is a two-edged sword, as it serves both perpetrators and victims of the Third Reich alike. In spite of that, or maybe because of that, the proverbial wealth of the *Diaries 1933-1945* is a sign of their linguistic and factual authenticity. As early as February 15, 1934, Victor Klemperer wrote with proverbial expressiveness "The truth speaks for itself" (I,87), and this is also expressed by the Biblical proverbial statement "I will bear witness to the last," written down by Klemperer on June 11, 1942, and ultimately chosen by the editors for the title of his *Diaries 1933-1945*. They are indeed particularly valuable documents of the proverbial *vox populi,* or better *voces populi,* of an infamous period in German history.

Notes:

A slightly shorter version of this lecture with the title "'Vox Populi - Voces Populi': Proverbial Revelations in Victor Klemperer's *Diaries of the Nazi Years (1933-1945)* has appeared in Wolfgang Mieder and David Scrase (eds.), *Reflections on the Holocaust. Festschrift for Raul Hilberg* (Burlington, Vermont: The Center for Holocaust Studies at the University of Vermont, 2001), pp. 99-120.

[1]See Eugen Seidel and Ingeborg Seidel-Slotty, *Sprachwandel im Dritten Reich* (Halle: Verlag Sprache und Literatur, 1961); Cornelia Berning, *Vom Abstammungsnachweis zum Zuchtwort: Vokabular des Nationalsozialismus* (Berlin: Walter de Gruyter, 1964); Siegfried Bork, *Mißbrauch der Sprache: Tendenzen nationalsozialistischer Sprachregelung* (München: Francke, 1970); Utz Maas, *Als der Geist der Gemeinschaft eine Sprache fand: Sprache im Nationalsozialismus. Versuch einer historischen Argumentationsanalyse* (Opladen: Westdeutscher Verlag, 1984); and Gerhard Bauer, *Sprache und Sprachlosigkeit im "Dritten Reich"* (Köln: Bund-Verlag, 1988).

[2]Heidrun Kämper, "Zeitgeschichte - Sprachgeschichte: Gedanken bei der Lektüre des Tagebuchs eines Philologen. Über die Ausgaben von Victor Klemperers Tagebuch 1933-1945," *Zeitschrift für Germanistische Linguistik,*

24 (1996), 328-341 (here p. 328 and 329).

[3]Rita Schober, "Sprache - Kultur - Humanismus: Victor Klemperer zum Gedenken," in: R. Schober, *Vom Sinn und Unsinn der Literaturwissenschaft* (Halle: Mitteldeutscher Verlag, 1988), pp. 181-204 (here p. 188).

[4]See Wolfgang Mieder, "Sprichwörter unterm Hakenkreuz," in: W. Mieder, *Deutsche Sprichwörter in Literatur, Politik, Presse und Werbung* (Hamburg: Helmut Buske, 1983), pp. 181 210. In English published as "Proverbs in Nazi Germany: The Promulgation of Anti-Semitism and Stereotypes Through Folklore," in: W. Mieder, *Proverbs Are Never Out of Season: Popular Wisdom in the Modern Age* (New York: Oxford University Press, 1993), pp. 225-255.

[5]Cited from Victor Klemperer, *Curriculum vitae. Erinnerungen 1881-1918*, ed. Walter Nowojski. 2 vols. (Berlin: Rütten & Loening, 1989; Berlin: Aufbau Taschenbuch Verlag, 1996), vol. 1, pp. 7-8.

[6]See Victor Klemperer, *Leben sammeln, nicht fragen wozu und warum. Tagebücher 1918-1932*, ed. Walter Nowojski. 2 vols. (Berlin: Aufbau-Verlag, 1996); and V. Klemperer, *So sitze ich denn zwischen allen Stühlen. Tagebücher 1945-1959*, ed. Walter Nowojski. 2 vols. (Berlin: Aufbau-Verlag, 1999). There is also the separately published volume by Victor Klemperer, *Und so ist alles schwankend. Tagebücher Juni bis Dezember 1945*, eds. Günter Jäckel and Hadwig Klemperer (Berlin: Aufbau Taschenbuch Verlag, 1995).

[7]See Volker Ullrich, "Der Chronist des Jahrhunderts. Mit Victor Klemperers Aufzeichnungen der Jahre 1945-1959 wird nun die Edition seiner Tagebücher abgeschlossen," *Die Zeit*, no. 13 (March 25, 1999), pp. 19-20.

[8]See in this context also the English contribution by Amos Elon, "The Jew [Victor Klemperer] Who Fought to Stay German," *The New York Times Magazine* (March 24, 1996), pp. 52-55.

[9]All volume and page numbers refer to Victor Klemperer, *Ich will Zeugnis ablegen bis zum letzten. Tagebücher 1933-1945*, ed. Walter Nowojski, 2 vols. (Berlin: Aufbau-Verlag, 1995). Where the English translation was available in print, the second set of volume and page numbers refers to the corresponding English translation. The instances labeled with a Roman number III are cited from Victor Klemperer, *Und so ist alles schwankend. Tagebücher Juni bis Dezember 1945*, eds. Günter Jäckel and Hadwig Klemperer (Berlin: Aufbau Taschenbuch Verlag, 1995). So far, only the first volume of the diaries is available in English translation by Martin Chalmers: *I Will Bear Witness: A Diary of the Nazi Years 1933-1941* (New York: Random House, 1998).

[10]Of course, Klemperer continued his cultural linguistic research after the war. It was as early as June 25, 1945, two months after the end of the war that he entered the following remark in his diary: "It is about time I started paying attention to the language of the FOURTH REICH. It does not seem to differ much from that of the THIRD, as different as Saxonian spoken in Dresden and Leipzig." (III,31). Almost two months later, we find the term L[ingua] Q[uartii] I[mperii] on August 16: "I don't see any difference between LTI and LQI" (III,94). And on October 12: "Every day I observe the continuation of LTI in LQI" (III,157), and three days later proverbially: "LQI just takes over LTI, bones and all" (III,159), up to October 26, where we find the equation "LTI=LQI" (III,168). See particularly Roderick H. Watt, "Victor Klemperer's 'Sprache des Vierten Reiches': LTI=LQI?" *German*

Life and Letters, 51 (1998), 360-371 (here pp. 367-369); Konrad Ehlich, "... 'LTI, LQI' ... - Von der Unschuld der Sprache und der Schuld der Sprechenden," in: *Das 20. Jahrhundert: Sprachgeschichte - Zeitgeschichte*, eds. Heidrun Kämper and Hartmut Schmidt (Berlin: Walter de Gruyter, 1998), pp. 275-303 (here pp. 287-289); Klaus-Dietmar Henke, "Mutmaßungen über Victor Klemperers Leben in zwei deutschen Diktaturen," in: *Leben in zwei Diktaturen: Victor Klemperers Leben in der NS-Zeit und in der DDR*, eds. Christoph Wielepp and Hans-Peter Lühr (Dresden: Friedrich-Ebert-Stiftung, 1998), pp. 15-19 (here p. 17); and Günter Jäckel, "'Zwiespältiger denn je': Dresden 1945 in Victor Klemperers Tagebuch," in: *Leben in zwei Dikataturen*, pp. 52-60 (here p. 55). The much earlier essay by Karl W. Fricke, "Die Sprache des Vierten Reiches," *Deutsche Rundschau*, 78 (1952), 1243-1246, is quite opinionated against the language conventions in East Germany and only refers to Klemperer's *LTI*.

[11]See for example Heidrun Kämper, "Zeitgeschichte - Sprachgeschichte," p. 329; M.H. Würzner, "Das Tagebuch als 'Oral History'," *Amsterdamer Beiträge zur älteren Germanistik*, 48 (1997), 169-173 (here p. 173); and Hans Reiss, "Victor Klemperer (1881-1960): Reflections on His 'Third Reich' Diaries," *German Life and Letters*, 51 (1998), 65-92 (here p. 84).

[12]With this sentence begins a speech presented by the East German author Fritz Rudolf Fries (who has since been accused of cooperation with the Stasi) on October 9, 1995, in the Leipzig opera. The 23 page speech was published as *Lesarten zu Klemperer* (Berlin: Aufbau-Verlag, 1996), here p. 5.

[13]Ewald Lang, "Victor Klemperers *LTI*," *Osnabrücker Beiträge zur Sprachtheorie*, 33 (1986), 69-79 (here p. 72); and Hans Helmut Christmann, "Victor Klemperer und sein 'Curriculum vitae'," in: *Literarhistorische Begegnungen. Festschrift Bernhard König*, eds. Andreas Kablitz and Ulrich Schulz-Buschhaus (Tübingen: Gunter Narr, 1993), pp. 17-28 (here p. 19).

[14]Heidrun Kämper, "Zeitgeschichte - Sprachgeschichte," p. 340; and Alexandra Przyrembel, "Die Tagebücher Victor Klemperers und ihre Wirkung in der deutschen Öffentlichkeit," in: *Geschichtswissenschaft und Öffentlichkeit. Der Streit um Daniel J. Goldhagen*, eds. Johannes Heil and Rainer Erb (Frankfurt am Main: Fischer Taschenbuch Verlag, 1998), pp. 312-327 (here p. 314).

[15]See Karl Friedrich Wilhelm Wander, *Deutsches Sprichwörter-Lexikon*, 5 vols. (Leipzig: F.A. Brockhaus, 1867-1880; Reprint Darmstadt: Wissenschaftliche Buchgesellschaft, 1964), vol. 4, col. 1051, "Tausend" no. 4. Klemperer's reference is also cited in Johannes Dirschauer, "Zur Faszination Victor Klemperers," in: *Leben in zwei Diktaturen: Viktor Klemperers Leben in der NS-Zeit und in der DDR*, eds. Christoph Wielepp and Hans-Peter Lühr (Dresden: Friedrich-Ebert-Stiftung, 1998), pp. 70-76 (p. 71); and by Henry Ashby Turner, "Victor Klemperer's Holocaust," *German Studies Review*, 22 (1999), 385-395 (here p. 386).

[16]See in this context Wolfgang Brückner, *"Arbeit macht frei": Herkunft und Hintergrund der KZ-Devise* (Opladen: Leske & Budrich, 1998); and Karin Doerr, "'To Each His Own' (Jedem das Seine): The (Mis)Use of German Proverbs in Concentration Camps and Beyond", *Proverbium*, 17 (2000), 71-90.

[17]Martin Walser, *Das Prinzip Genauigkeit. Laudatio auf Victor Klemperer* (Frankfurt am Main: Suhrkamp, 1996), p. 53. This essay is also printed in Martin

Walser, *Literatur als Weltverständnis. Drei Versuche* (Eggingen: Edition Isele, 1996), pp. 19-58 (here p. 58).

[18]See also the 65 variations of the proverb "In vino veritas" or "Im Wein ist (liegt) Wahrheit" for the period between 1650 and 1995 in Wolfgang Mieder (ed.), *Verdrehte Weisheiten: Antisprichwörter aus Literatur und Medien* (Wiesbaden: Quelle & Meyer, 1998), pp. 311-318.

[19]Victor Klemperer, *LTI. Notizbuch eine Philologen* (Köln: Röderberg, 1987), p. 16. On this section of the *LTI*-book see also Utz Maas, "Eine Bewährungsprobe für die Sprachwissenschaft: Sprache im Nationalsozialismus und ihre Analyse [von Victor Klemperer]," in U. Maas, *"Als der Geist der Gemeinschaft eine Sprache fand": Sprache im Nationalsozialismus. Versuch einer historischen Argumentationsanalyse* (Opladen: Westdeutscher Verlag, 1984), pp. 208-219 (here p. 216); and Hans Reiss, "Victor Klemperer," p. 75. The German language edition of the book with many helpful English annotations should also be mentioned: *An Annotated Edition of Victor Klemperer's "LTI": Notizbuch eines Philologen*, ed. Roderick H. Watt (Lewiston, New York: Edwin Mellen Press, 1997).

[20]On the role of fairy tales in the Third Reich see Christa Kamenetsky, *Children's Literature in Hitler's Germany: The Cultural Policy of National Socialism* (Athens, Ohio: Ohio University Press, 1984); and Wolfgang Mieder, "Language and Folklore of the Holocaust," in: David Scrase and W. Mieder (eds.), *The Holocaust: Introductory Essays* (Burlington, Vermont: The Center for Holocaust Studies at the University of Vermont, 1996), pp. 93-106.

[21]The Grimm fairy tale and the Chamisso poem are printed in Wolfgang Mieder (ed.), *Deutsche Sprichwörter und Redensarten* (Stuttgart: Philipp Reclam, 1979), pp. 39-41 and pp. 79-81.

[22]Viktor Klemperer, *LTI*, p. 166 and p. 167.

[23]Rita Schober, "Sprache - Kultur - Humanismus," p. 190; and Bärbel Techtmeier, "Bedeutung zwischen Wort und Tat: Die Sprache des Faschismus im Spiegel von Victor Klemperers 'LTI'," in: *Bedeutungen und Ideen in Sprachen und Texten*, eds. Werner Neumann and B. Techtmeier (Berlin: Akademie-Verlag, 1987), pp. 315-324 (here p. 321).

[24]See Jürgen Fuchs, "Das Erschrecken über die eigene Sprache," *Deutsche Akademie für Sprache und Dichtung*, no volume given (1983), 42-53 (here p. 42); and Utz Maas, "Eine Bewährungsprobe für die Sprachwissenschaft," p. 209.

[25]See also Wolfgang Mieder, "'Make Hell While the Sun Shines': Proverbial Rhetoric in Winston Churchill's *The Second World War*," in: W. Mieder, *The Politics of Proverbs*, pp. 39-66; and W. Mieder and George B. Bryan, *The Proverbial Winston S. Churchill: An Index to Proverbs in the Works of Sir Winston Churchill* (Westport, Connecticut: Greenwood Press, 1995).

[26]See Raul Hilberg, *The Destruction of the European Jews* (Chicago: Quadrangle Books, 1961); also in German translation by Christian Seeger, Harry Maor, Walle Bengs, and Wilfried Szepan under the title *Die Vernichtung der europäischen Juden*, 3 vols. (Frankfurt am Main: Fischer Taschenbuch Verlag, 1990); and R. Hilberg, *Perpetrators, Victims, Bystanders: The Jewish Catastrophe 1933-1945* (New York: Harper Collins, 1992); translated into German by Hans Günter Holl under the title *Täter, Opfer, Zuschauer: Die Vernichtung der Juden 1933-1945* (Frankfurt am Main: S. Fischer, 1992).

[27]Karl Kraus, *Aphorismen*, ed. Christian Wagenknecht (Frankfurt am Main: Suhrkamp, 1986), p. 159. For 19 further variations of this quotation, see Wolfgang Mieder (ed.), *Ver-kehrte Worte: Antizitate aus Literatur und Medien* (Wiesbaden: Quelle & Meyer, 1997), pp. 322-325.

[28]See particularly Lawrence Birken, "Prussianism, Nazism, and Romanticism in the Thought of Victor Klemperer," *German Quarterly*, 72 (1999), 33-43.

[29]Victor Klemperer, *LTI*, pp. 230-231. This text is also cited by Margret and Siegfried Jäger in "Victor Klemperers Sprach- und Kulturkritik," p. 45.

[30]See the many instances gathered in Wolfgang Mieder, *"Morgenstunde hat Gold im Munde": Studien und Belege zum populärsten deutschsprachigen Sprichwort* (Wien: Edition Praesens, 1997); and W. Mieder, *Verdrehte Weisheiten*, pp. 198-207.

[31]Cited from Max Domarus, *Hitler. Reden und Proklamationen 1932 bis 1945*, 2 vols. (Neustadt a.d. Aisch: Schmidt, 1962), vol. 1, p. 248 and 251.

[32]See also Victor Klemperer, *LTI*, pp. 39-40.

[33]See also Victor Klemperer, *LTI*, p. 38.

[34]Victor Klemperer, *LTI*, pp. 190-191. On this joke on the expression "to keep one's word to someone" see also this bitter statement from August 11, 1935: "Pflugk told me: They say they haven't kept their word to anyone, except the Jews!" (I,213).

[35]See also the principal study by Raul Hilberg, *Die Vernichtung der europäischen Juden*, 3 vols. (Frankfurt am Main: Fischer Taschenbuch Verlag, 1990). First published in English as *The Destruction of the European Jews* (Chicago: Quadrangle Books, 1961).

[36]Max Domarus, *Hitler. Reden und Proklamationen*, vol. 2, p. 1937.

[37]Max Domarus, *Hitler. Reden und Proklamationen*, vol. 2, pp. 1828-1829.

[38]See Julius Schwab, *Rassenpflege im Sprichwort. Eine volkstümliche Sammlung* (Leipzig: Alwin Fröhlich, 1937); and Ernst Hiemer, *Der Jude im Sprichwort der Völker* (Nürnberg: Der Stürmer, 1942).

[39]This statement appears almost identically in Victor Klemperer, *LTI*, p. 35.

[40]Since the two volumes of the *Diaries 1933-1945* unfortunately do not contain an index, some references to concentration camps are noted here: KZ (general): II,260, 284, 355 and 509; Auschwitz II,47, 268, 312 and 355; Buchenwald I,443 and 578; Dachau II,748; and Theresienstadt II,151, 160 and 491.

[41]Victor Klemperer, "Einprägen!," in: *Victor Klemperer zum Gedenken von seinen Freunden und ihm selbst*, ed. F. Zschech (Rudolstadt: Greifenverlag, 1961), pp. 162-165 (here p. 165).

[42]Jan Philipp Reemtsma, "'Buchenwald wird von andern geschildert werden; ich will mich an meine Erlebnisse halten': Stenogramme aus der Vorhölle," in: *Im Herzen der Finsternis: Victor Klemperer als Chronist der NS-Zeit*, ed. Hannes Heer (Berlin: Aufbau-Verlag, 1997), pp. 170-193 (here S. 170); and Alexandra Przyrembel, "Die Tagebücher Victor Klemperers," p. 313.

[43]See also Hans-Manfred Militz, "Redewendungen im '*LTI*' von Victor Klemperer," pp. 214-215. On the proverb itself see G. Boas, *Vox Populi: Essays in the History of an Idea* (Baltimore, Maryland: Johns Hopkins University Press, 1969), pp. 3-38.

[44]Max Domarus, *Hitler. Reden und Proklamationen*, vol. 1, p. 607.

[45]Victor Klemperer, *LTI*, p. 236 and 248.

[46]Victor Klemperer, *LTI*, p. 168. In his pamphlet *Zur gegenwärtigen Sprach-situation in Deutschland* (Berlin: Aufbau-Verlag, 1953), Klemperer makes a similar statement: "In the language of a nation, its entire heritage is contained, it belongs to all as a common heritage and it informs all" (p. 6).

[47]See the short statements made by Heidrun Kämper, "Zeitgeschichte - Sprachgeschichte," p. 339; Hans Reiss, "Victor Klemperer," p. 84; and Margret and Siegfried Jäger, "Victor Klemperers Sprach- und Kulturkritik," p. 55.

[48]M.H. Würzner, "Das Tagebuch als 'Oral History'," p. 170 and 172.

[49]See Daniel J. Goldhagen, *Hitler's Willing Executioners: Ordinary Germans and the Holocaust* (New York: Alfred A. Knopf, 1996). Translated into German by Klaus Kochmann under the title *Hitlers willige Vollstrecker: Ganz gewöhnliche Deutsche und der Holocaust* (Berlin: Siedler, 1996). On the controversy around Goldhagen's book see Julius H. Schoeps (ed.), *Ein Volk von Mördern? Die Dokumentation zur Goldhagen-Kontroverse um die Rolle der Deutschen im Holocaust* (Hamburg: Hoffmann und Campe, 1996); Raul Hilberg, "The Goldhagen Phenomenon," *Critical Inquiry*, 23 (1997), 721-728; and Johannes Heil and Rainer Erb (eds.), *Geschichtswissenschaft und Öffentlichkeit: Der Streit um Daniel J. Goldhagen* (Frankfurt am Main: Fischer Taschenbuch Verlag, 1998).

[50]See the insightful contribution of Hannes Heer, "Vox populi: Zur Mentalität der Volksgemeinschaft," in: *Im Herzen der Finsternis: Victor Klemperer als Chronist der NS-Zeit*, ed. H. Heer (Berlin: Aufbau-Verlag, 1997), pp. 122-143.

[51]See also the following statement made on July 20, 1941: "Will anyone ever collect those secret, dangerous jokes of the Hitler era? They are part of LTI" (I,640).

[52]See Alan Dundes and Thomas Hauschild, "Auschwitz Jokes," *Western Folklore*, 42 (1983), 249-260; and A. Dundes and T. Hauschild, "Kennt der Witz kein Tabu? Zynische Erzählformen als Versuch der Bewältigung national-sozialistischer Verbrechen," *Zeitschrift für Volkskunde*, 83 (1987), 21-31.

[53]See Karl S. Guthke, "Lessing and the Jews," in: *Shifting Paradigms in German-Jewish Relations (1750-2000). Harry H. Kahn Memorial Lectures (1995-1999)*, eds. Wolfgang Mieder and Hazel Kahn Keimowitz (Burlington, Vermont: Center for Holocaust Studies at the University of Vermont, 1999), pp. 35-58.

[54]See Victor Klemperer, *LTI*, p. 60.

[55]Heidrun Kämper, "Zeitgeschichte - Sprachgeschichte," p. 330. This reference is also mentioned by Hans Reiss, "Victor Klemperer," p. 85. See also Kurt Nemitz, "Victor Klemperer und die jüdische Alltagsexistenz im NS-Staat 1933 bis 1941," in: *Leben in zwei Diktaturen: Victor Klemperers Leben in der NS-Zeit und in der DDR*, eds. Chrisoph Wielepp and Hans-Peter Lühr (Dresden: Friedrich-Ebert-Stiftung, 1998), pp. 28-38 (here p. 34).

[56]See also Klemperer's proverbial statement of July 21, 1935: "My principles about Germans and other nationalities have become as shaky as an old man's teeth" (I,211).

[57]On this proverb see P.J. Vinken, "Some Observations on the Symbolism of 'The Broken Pot' in Art and Literature," *American Imago*, 15 (1958), 149-174; and Gisela Zick, "Der zerbrochene Krug als Bildmotiv des 18. Jahrhunderts," *Wallraf-Richartz Jahrbuch*, 31 (1969), 149-204.

Separate Realities:
Jewish and Gentile Representations of the Holocaust

Dagmar C.G. Lorenz

Introduction

The twelfth Harry H. Kahn Memorial Lecture was delivered on April 27, 2001, and we were glad to welcome Prof. Dagmar C.G. Lorenz from the University of Illinois at Chicago as our distinguished speaker. She had been scheduled to present this lecture the previous year, but a snowstorm prevented her from making the trip to wintry Vermont.

It is a special honor to welcome our well-known colleague and good friend Prof. Dagmar C.G. Lorenz to the campus of the University of Vermont this afternoon. As some of you will remember, Prof. Lorenz was prevented from speaking to us last year by a late snowstorm, but today she is definitely here with us. Prof. Lorenz finished her undergraduate studies in 1970 with a double major in English and German at the University of Göttingen in Germany. She then earned two M.A. degrees in German and English from the University of Cincinnati in Ohio, and it is also this university that awarded her the Ph.D. degree in 1974. She then worked for almost twenty-five years as a professor of German at Ohio State University, where Harry Kahn had been a Ph.D. student many years earlier. In 1998 Prof. Lorenz moved on to the University of Illinois at Chicago, where she is presently the editor of the prestigious *German Quarterly*, the flagship journal in the field of German with over 7000 subscribers. Her editorship is a clear indication of her high esteem in the German profession. Little wonder that she has recently been invited as guest professor to the University of Cincinnati and Washington University in St. Louis. It would certainly be an honor if we could have Prof. Lorenz on our campus for a semester sometime in the future.

Prof. Lorenz is a specialist, both as a teacher and scholar, in Austrian literature, women's literature, film studies, Jewish authors writing in German, and the Holocaust. While she has taught and published in these multifaceted areas, there is no doubt that Prof. Lorenz is one of the most eminent scholars on Anti-Semitism and the Holocaust as they are represented in Austrian and German literature. Her article on "Holocaust-Literatur als Teil des Lehrplans in der deutschen Abteilung einer amerikanischen Universität" (1994) reveals her serious commitment to the teaching of the Holocaust to American students, something that is also a major goal of the Center for Holocaust Studies here at the University of Vermont. This same didactic interest can be seen from her invaluable articles in such encyclopedias as *The Feminist Encyclopedia of German Literature* (1997), the *Yale Companion to Jewish Writing and Thought in German Culture* (1997), and also *Women Writer's in German-Speaking Countries* (1998).

This is not the place and time to cite all the publications which this untiring scholar has brought out in the past twenty-five years. A computer search of her scholarly activities reveals a multitude of intriguing papers and books that have appeared in the German or English language on such authors as Adalbert Stifter, Franz Grillparzer, Theodor Fontane, Joseph Roth, Marieluise Fleisser, Elke Lasker-Schüler, Friedrich Torberg, Gertrud Kolmar, Erich Fried, Ilse Aichinger, and many others. Naturally I can mention only some of the most significant articles here, as for example "Elfriede Jelinek's Political Feminism" (1990), "Austrian Jewish History and Identity after 1945" (1994), "Anti-Semitism in the Tradition of German Discourse: The Path to the Holocaust" (1995), "Das antiheroische Ethos in der deutsch-jüdischen Literatur" (1995), "The Pluralist Paradigm: The Anti-Idealism of Austrian Literature" (1996), "Jewish Women Authors and the Exile Experience: Claire Goll, Veza Canetti, Else Lasker-Schüler, Nelly Sachs, Cordelia Edvardson" (1998), "In Search of the Land of the Fathers: Galicia, the Bukovina and Eastern European Jewry in the Works of Contemporary German and Austrian Authors and Filmmakers" (1998), and "Holocaust Literature and Films as Crime Fiction" (1998). And there are also several valuable books and edited volumes, among them such standard works as *Aesthetics and Politics of Fascism: West German Women Filmmakers in the Nineteen Seventies* (1988), *Insiders and Outsiders: Jewish and Gentile Culture in Germany and Austria* (1994), *Transforming the Center, Eroding the Margins: Essays on Ethnic and Cultural Boundaries in German-Speaking Countries* (1998), and *Contemporary Jewish Writing in Austria: An Anthology* (1999). In these books Prof. Lorenz also shows that she is a superb translator of both scholarly and poetic publications.But let me close these introductory remarks by mentioning two very special books which Prof. Lorenz has written in the broad area of Holocaust studies, namely *Verfolgung bis zum Massenmord: Holocaust-Diskurse in deutscher Sprache aus der Sicht der Verfolgten* (1992) and *Keepers of the Motherland: German Texts by Jewish Women Writers* (1997). These books have already become "classic" works, and they will certainly be read and appreciated by generations of students and scholars interested in how language and literature might help to get a better understanding of the Holocaust and its aftermath.

Prof. Lorenz has dedicated more than two decades to the engaged study of the Holocaust, and she is one of the pioneers among German professors in this country who decided that the teaching of the Holocaust must be part of any German program at colleges and universities. As a teacher she has helped her students to gain new insights into this terrible tragedy, and as a scholar she has provided us with invaluable resources and interpretations of the Holocaust. For all of this dedicated and committed work we owe much thanks and appreciation to Prof. Dagmar C.G. Lorenz.

Lecture

Separate Versions of History. Positionality and What is Important to Recount

Texts about the Nazi era, World War II and the Holocaust by Jewish and non-Jewish Germans read as if they were set in a different time at a different place. Critical assessments differ as well. For example, Jewish critics question the moral right of the

survivors of Stalingrad and Dresden to put their suffering on a
par with that of the survivors of Theresienstadt and Auschwitz
and Holocaust deniers dispute the official version of 20th century
history. Historically speaking the matter seems simple enough.
Germans—although not all Germans—made it possible for the
National Socialists to ascend to power in 1933, and even though
there was resistance, it was not strong enough to shatter Nazi
power from within. The advantages promised and provided by
the regime, including medals for mothers, speedy promotions in
the SS, and access to the property of deported Jews, prompted
many initially reluctant Germans to endorse National Socialism
further along the line. There were virtually no protests against
the disenfranchisement of Jewish Germans, let alone Jews classi-
fied as stateless or Jews outside of Germany, and there has been
massive resistance against facing up to the genocide after the
war. One can only speculate why that was. Could it have been
the repressed guilt and shame, as Alexander and Margarete
Mitscherlich assumed or, more likely, that the persecution of the
Jews, preached throughout the ages long before Hitler, was
viewed as unspectacular, if not as a matter-of-course, in a society
thoroughly indoctrinated with visions of its own superiority. The
inferiority of other races and cultures and the destructiveness of
the so-called Jews, whether they were Jewish by religion, culture
or descent was a given, regardless as to whether the targets of
Nazi hatred identified themselves as Jews.

Warriors and Victims

Paradigmatic of the insensitivity toward Jewish suffering and
the indifference toward anyone not German on the part of German mainstream writers is the radio play *Draußen vor der Tür*
(The Man Outside), written in 1946 by the veteran Wolfgang
Borchert. The protagonist, Beckmann, has just returned from a
Soviet POW camp and embodies German suffering. In the sur-
real setting of a morality play the ordeal of the defeated German
soldier is staged as *theatrum mundi*, *Welttheater*. Among the allegorical figures summoned are no other than God, Death, and
the Elbe river. Their emergence underscores the cosmic dimen-
sions of the average German's tragedy after the collapse of his
world. In an eerie postwar landscape Beckmann encounters peo-

ple and a country he no longer recognizes, and who no longer want him.

From the point of view of the former Nazi soldier, Borchert's Germany has abandoned her loyal sons. Every one of Borchert's characters with the exception of the veteran, the emblem of the average man, has adjusted to the changed conditions. Beckmann, in his inability to conform, comes across as a man of integrity. The motif of the harlot, represented by Beckmann's wife who lives with another man, and the woman who picks Beckmann up is also present in the behavior of the postwar Germans who repudiate the past and the Nazi soldier.

Borchert's focal theme is the undoing of the young men who sacrificed themselves for the Nazi cause and whom the defeated fatherland left unrewarded. The play indicts the Germans who became "denazified" and went on with their lives. Borchert's hero is the unrehabilitated Nazi soldier, the villains in the play are the unfaithful wife, the colonel for whom the war was just a job rather than a cause, the cabaret director who does not want to be bothered with the soldier's tales of woe, and Frau Kramer who has taken over the apartment of Beckmann's parents who, as it transpires, just recently committed suicide because the postwar authorities held them accountable for old Mr. Beckmann's antisemitic activities.

Borchert's audience is called upon to sympathize with the old Nazis who turned on the gas stove just because old Mr. Beckmann was "a bit too active" and "could not take the Jews. They stimulated his bile."[1] Young Beckmann was obviously aware of and possibly shared his father's convictions—the rather unpleasant Mrs. Kramer underscores "but you knew all that, you, his son"—but none of this is a cause for concern. The only gassing mentioned in *Draußen vor der Tür* is that of the old Nazis, the only innocent victim is a Wehrmacht veteran. German suffering is the only suffering that matters, German lives are the only ones that count. The only guilt issue raised is Beckmann's guilty conscience because German soldiers lost their lives while he was in command.

Postwar writers such as Borchert portray the end of the war as the Point Zero, the total collapse and *tabula rasa*. They call for a reform of the German language and a new culture. The radical terms in which they describe the Zero Hour calls to mind the Nazi rhetoric of totality—the total war and total destruction. Borchert's manifesto opens with the words "Helm ab, Helm ab:—wir haben verloren" (Helmet off, helmet off, we have lost)[2] and sets in on a pacifist note. Toward the end, however, it is obvious that the nationalist fervor is anything but overcome. Cast ing himself and his generation as protesters, "nay-sayers," and "nihilists" who must transform nothingness into renewed affirmation, he professes his and his peers' love for "this gigantic desert called Germany." "We" and all like "us," he writes, want to survive for the love of Germany which "we love like the Christians love their Christ: Because of her suffering."[3] Among those Borchert lists as deserving love for the sake of their suffering are mothers who filled bomb shells, demoralized war heroes, raped women, and the common soldiers who tell their story to their grandchildren.

Borchert's themes are characteristic of the way the war and the postwar era are portrayed in German literature and film in the decades to come. The character of the defeated German soldier on the fringes of the economic boom occurs in Sanders-Brahms's *Deutschland bleiche Mutter* and Fassbinder's *Die Ehe der Maria Braun*. The latter also features the cold-hearted promiscuous woman as a symbol of the commercialization of German culture. Sanders-Brahms's film represents German women as the victims of recent history, as does Peter Handke in *Wuschloses Unglück.* Typically, these works do not deal with the Holocaust or contain only sporadic allusions as is the case in *Deutschland bleiche Mutter.* Here one episode shows the protagonist Lene and her friend witnessing the arrest of their Jewish neighbors from a window. Alarmed by the sound of shattering glass they look out, scared. Against Lene's faint protest that their friend Rachel is taken away, the other woman closes the curtains. In another scene Lene takes yarn from a store formerly owned by deported Jews, and a more extensive episode places her and her daughter into a setting that calls to mind a death camp. In all instances Sanders-Brahms's protagonist opts to ignore the significance of what she sees. Her own misery, her husband's sudden brutality toward her, the bombing, the loss of her home, and finally the rape by American soldiers counterbalance the allusions to the Shoah which this film released in 1979, one year after the

airing of the TV series *Holocaust*, could not leave unacknowledged.

The works of German and Austrian mainstream writers of
the war and postwar generations prioritize Gentile experiences
and perceptions. This is also the case in Brigitte Schwaiger's
autobiographical novel *Lange Abwesenheit* (1980) which juxta-
poses an Austrian and a Jew, the female protagonist/narrator's
father and friend Birer, who has become her lover.[4] By associat-
ing herself with the much older Jewish man the protagonist seeks
to compensate for the tenderness her antisemitic father has de-
nied her. The father's death resolves the conflict—the protagonist finds a dead father easier to love than a living one—Birer,
who is portrayed in unflattering terms throughout the novel, becomes expendable.

These few examples illustrate the self-centered focus of
German and Austrian representations of the genocide and post-
Shoah conflicts. The dominant perspective precludes a more than
fleeting awareness of the suffering inflicted upon non-German
populations. By foregrounding characters unlikely to have played a major role in the Nazi era—low-ranking soldiers, house-
wives, and perhaps children of Nazis—the issue of responsibility
is successfully downplayed. Within these parameters German-
centered narratives unfold, complete with episodes from the everyday lives of ordinary people: childhood experiences, romance,
marriage, and friendships. Among these the war represents a dis-
ruptive and potentially tragic interlude but also an adventure, as
is the case in Handke, Fassbinder, and Sanders-Brahms.[5]

Jewish Memory

Holocaust memoirs, fiction and films by Jewish authors have
different protagonists and portray the Nazi era in fundamentally
different terms. The mere mention of Germany instills painful
memories, all the more so since many German-Jewish writers
remained deeply identified with their native country. Borchert's
suffering German soldiers and civilians are the other, the enemy
in Jewish writing. Autobiographical novels such as *Die größere
Hoffnung* by Ilse Aichinger, who survived in Vienna in a somewhat privileged situation and later in hiding, and *Schwester der
Nacht* by the Auschwitz survivor Peter Edel, the diary of Anne

Frank, and films like Peter Lilienthal's and Jurek Becker's *David* reveal that since the beginning of the war at the very latest the Jewish experience was one of unspeakable deprivation and persecution.[6] The days were filled with activities designed to ensure survival on the most basic level.

This is all the more true for prisoners in ghettos and concentration camps. Their reality bore no resemblance to peace time living. The horrendous conditions in the concentration camps and ghettos are portrayed in the works of Edgar Hilsenrath, Jurek Becker and Gerty Spies. This world, in the words of Ruth Klüger who survived Theresienstadt and Auschwitz, "felt like a crater of the moon, a place only peripherally connected with the human world. It is this 'otherness' of the death camps that we have such difficulty conveying. But once the killing stopped, these former camps became a piece of our inhabited earth again."[7]

The memories of Jewish survivors, whether they had been in hiding, exile, or prisoners in the camps, cast a shadow over their lives long after the liberation and along with the mourning of family members and friends prevented their lives from becoming "normal" again. The poet Paul Celan never ceased being preoccupied with the Holocaust in spiritual and poetic terms. He committed suicide in 1970. The Auschwitz survivor Jean Améry who killed himself in 1978 reflected upon the lasting effects of the complete helplessness under torture.[8]

The Nobel Prize winning poet Nelly Sachs had escaped her scheduled deportation by a hair's breadth. Living in Swedish exile she was consumed by the Jewish fate under Nazism. Similar to Borchert's *Draußen vor der Tür* her drama *Eli. Ein Mysterienspiel vom Leiden Israels* is cosmic theater about the issues of guilt, responsibility, and revenge. Like Borchert, Sachs introduces allegorical and elemental forces such as the *Sch'ma Israel*, the Jewish prayer in praise of God's greatness, the chimneys of the death camps, and Michael, God's deputy and avenger. Her protagonist is the Jewish people, represented by Eastern European Jewish survivors, simple people calling to mind Chagall's paintings and Buber's *Hasidic Tales*. They have returned to their destroyed shtetl to mourn the dead and rebuild their community. The piety, humility and trust in God's wisdom in Sachs stands in stark contrast to the loss of faith in *Draußen vor der Tür* where God appears as a powerless old man confronted by a triumphant

Death, overfed and overbearing. Sachs's language is a tribute to the Yiddish language, the language of Eastern European Jewry whose culture Nazi Germany had destroyed.

Borchert and Sachs thematize a new beginning after the war. *Eli* celebrates the end of terror, murders and rapes, while mourning the destruction of the community. While the underlying emotions in *Draußen vor der Tür,* on the other hand, are frustration, disappointment, resentment, and anger. The very moment that ends the ordeal of Sachs's ordinary heroes and restores a semblance of normalcy seals the defeat of Borchert's soldier. Beckmann has to face the loss of his son, abandonment by his wife, and rejection by the new society. In fact, Sachs's perpetrator who succumbs to divine justice is also a "little" man, not unlike Beckmann. He is a shoemaker and the father of a son. The child's hostility toward the angelic Michael suggests that the boy, too, is thoroughly indoctrinated with antisemitism. While Borchert focusses on the plight of the common soldier facing cynicism and despair, Sachs reveals the insidiousness of the way the murderer of the Jews conducts his life, his brutality and spiritual emptiness. The murderer's punishment occurs without human interference or actions taken by Michael. Eli's murderer perishes through cosmic forces. Confessing his deeds—as did the commandant of Auschwitz Rudolf Hoess in the memoirs he wrote in his Cracow prison cell—Sachs's perpetrator hopes to elude punishment but he is instantly dissolved into nothingness.[9]

Sachs's poetic universe is Jewish by its setting, language and protagonists. Jewish characters and practices unfamiliar to most German and Austrian writers are central. The precise identity of the murderer, although most likely German, remains unspecified—it is irrelevant. Showcased is instead the violence of the Gentiles in contrast to the pacifism of the Hasidic Jews who remain true to their tradition. The murderer, on the other hand, kills without cause. The Jews, even if they can and by human law may be entitled to do so, will not kill. Non-violence is, in fact, one of Sachs's primary issues. Some of the shtetl boys, however, give rise to alarm. Impressed by what they have witnessed, they want to reenact acts of violence rather than playing peaceful games. They reveal the poet's concerns regarding the impact of the Holocaust for future generations of Jews.

Many motifs in Sachs's play are characteristic of post-Shoah Jewish writing, including the distinction between victims and perpetrators, the reflections upon guilt, punishment, and which position to assume toward the perpetrators and postwar Germany. Also characteristic is the portrayal of traditional Jewish life at a time when Jewish identity and the future of Jewish culture were threatened as never before. So is the representation of suffering while affirming life. The latter, as the filmmaker Nadja Seelich commented in connection with her film *Theresienstadt sah aus wie ein Curort,* was a psychological necessity for the survivors.[10] Contrary to the suicidal atmosphere in the works of Borchert and other veterans, the horrors described by Holocaust survivors rarely diminish the resolve to live.

Nazi anti-Semitism and the Holocaust brought about separate realities for Jews and Germans in terms of perception and actual experience. The Nazi regime ended the approximately two hundred year long history of emancipation and assimilation in German-speaking countries.

Until the Nazi takeover, and for many Jewish Germans for a long time thereafter, Jews and non-Jews in Germany and Austria had had similar expectations of life as well as common cultural and political ideals that derived from a shared socialization at school, at the university, at the workplace and through holidays and national events. World War I had been an important factor in mainstreaming Jewish Germans.[11] While the term "German-Jewish symbiosis," often applied to the Jewish situation in pre-Nazi German and Austrian society, seems overly idealistic because it evokes a hybrid culture of equal partners, it is true that many Jews had a profound affinity for German culture. Personalities as different as Rosa Luxemburg and Bertha Pappenheim, Joseph Roth and Elias Canetti are a case in point. Countless Jewish exiles and Holocaust survivors born before the Shoah, just to name Paul Celan, Hilde Spiel, Berthold Viertel, Gerty Spies, Edgar Hilsenrath, Ruth Klüger and, again, Canetti, remained attached to the German language and preoccupied with German culture. Despite the traumas of persecution, displacement, and the concentration camp experience many Jewish authors continued to define themselves through the German language. Their work connects them with the culture of their youth which at the same time is the culture of those who designed to destroy them and their history.

Modes of Representation: The Sentimental and the Grotesque

No event has had a more profound impact on contemporary German-speaking societies than the Holocaust. Ruth Klüger observes the term "most recent past" (jüngste Vergangenheit) is still today understood as a reference to the Nazi era. But the cultural memories differ greatly. Hans Thalberg, an Austrian Jewish diplomat, writes that the memories of Jews and non-Jews seem separated by a deep moat. These differences have become even more pronounced in the post-Shoah generations. The Christian author Albrecht Goes's assessesment of 1954 could not be further from the truth:

> Ach, in die Luft schreibt, wer ihrer gedenkt, ihrer deren irdisches Teil vergangen ist, Staub und Asche in Erde und Wind. Man hat vergessen. Und es muß ja auch vergessen werden, denn wie könnte leben, wer nicht vergessen kann?[12]

In 1989 the Jewish critic Ruth Beckermann, far from forgetting, writes:

> Die Kinder der Überlebenden sind dagegen nicht mehr bereit, still zu sein, mit Antisemiten zu diskutieren oder um Mitleid zu werben.[13]

And in 1999 Ernestine Bradley Schlant notes: "To succumb to a moral or aesthetic imperative that demands the silence of the Holocaust would be tantamount to acknowledging the very barbarism of which Auschwitz stands as the horrifying exemplar."[14]

Gentile authors often assume a tone of awe and mystery when writing about the Holocaust. Jewish writing often resorts to the grotesque and black humor to portray the monstrosity of the Nazi crimes. Many Jewish authors do so in deliberate intertextuality with Jewish writing of the early twentieth century, satire and cabaret that employ the grotesque and macabre, black humor, and cartoon-like characters—Elias Canetti, Karl Kraus, Jura Soyfer, Karl Farkas, Hermann Leopoldi, and Georg Kreisler. Jakov Lind, Edgar Hilsenrath and Elfriede Jelinek have continued this tradition, so have more recently yet Robert Schindel and Doron Rabinovici.

Lind and Hilsenrath use the satiric mode to deal with the Holocaust and Nazi crimes. The central episodes in Lind's *Soul of Wood* are set in the Viennese asylum *Unter Sankt Veit* where under the auspices of the euthanasia program disabled persons are murdered. Rather than depicting the man who administers the deadly injections as a dehumanized killing machine, Lind's World War I veteran Hermann Wohlbrecht is an ambivalent character. Socially marginal, like many who helped persecuted Jews, Wohlbrecht is a victim and a victimizer, a killer and a murder victim.[15] He helps the paralyzed Jew Anton Barth—not without self-interest, to be sure. After the deportation of Anton's parents he takes the boy to a mountain hide-out and leaves him there. Far away from civilization Anton experiences freedom for the first time. At the end of the war he becomes an alibi Jew for high-ranking Nazis.

Hilsenrath's novel *Der Nazi und der Friseur* also explores Nazi crimes and criminals. Max Schulz, the protagonist, is a mass murderer. Once his killer instincts are awakened during *Kristallnacht*, he goes on a rampage that lasts through the war and the beginnings of the state of Israel.[16] Schulz who had his boyhood friend Itzig Finkelstein and the entire Finkelstein family exterminated assumes the name Finkelstein and turns into a Jewish freedom fighter and a model Israeli.

There could be no greater contrast than between the Christian author Albrecht Goes's sanctimonious style and the crude and brutal comments of Hilsenrath's narrator:

> Kennen Sie das Konzentrationslager Laubwalde? Der Ort hatte früher einen polnischen Namen. Aber wir tauften ihn um: Laubwalde! Ein wunderschöner Ort umringt von Wald. In Laubwalde waren 200 000 Juden. Wir haben sie alle umgebracht. 200 000! Trotzdem war das ein kleines Lager, denn die meisten Gefangenen wurden gleich nach ihrer Einlieferung kaltgemacht. Das war praktisch. Denn auf diese Weise hatten wir nie zu viele von ihnen zu überwachen. (55)

> Seit Monaten denk' ich darüber nach, wie ich am besten untertauchen soll . . . und je mehr ich nachdenke, desto

öfter sag ich zu mir: 'Max Schulz! Wenn es ein zweites
Leben für dich gibt, dann solltest du es als Jude leben'
Und schließlich . . . wir haben den Krieg verloren. Und
die Juden haben ihn gewonnen. Und ich, Max Schulz,
war immer ein Idealist.' (125-6)

Not surprisingly, readers and critics in search of higher
meaning took offense at Hilsenrath's and Lind's plots, their provocative images, and their use of obscenity. German-speaking
audiences, uncomfortable with the past to begin with, reacted
with indignation to Holocaust satire. Perhaps because the laughter Lind's and Hilsenrath's texts evoke appeals to hidden impulses and confronts the readers with their own unacknowledged
complicity with the Nazis. Lind and Hilsenrath write to bring repressed memories to the surface, to make the reader feel like a
voyeur. Their novels play with taboos, expose greed and hypocrisy, uncover sadistic impulses, and reproduce the psycho-sexual
pleasure agents of the Nazi regime must have felt when they
acted as masters over life and death. *Eine Seele aus Holz* and
Der Nazi und der Friseur excite the readers and put them to
shame. They cause readers and audiences to experience the Nazi
within themselves.

Yet, the German-speaking public preferred to experience
their compassionate and noble side. "Evoking a sentimental response as did the dramatization of Anne Frank's Diary in the fif-
ties or the American television soap-opera hit *Holocaust*"[17] was
considered appropriate to the topic of the Shoah. Macabre works
were unsettling to audiences looking for happy endings and
celebrations of the human spirit. Lind and Hilsenrath were pioneers in creating a decanonized Holocaust literature that
"breaches the holiest taboos to redeem them through the gut-
ter."[18]

The rejection of satirical and grotesque literature by survivors on the part of a non-Jewish public (after the Shoah the per-
centage of Jews in Germany and Austria was approximately 0.1
%) raises the issue of positionality. Who, if anyone, has the right
to use satire in a work about the Holocaust? Is the only acceptable humor in a Holocaust text that of a supposedly life-
affirming kind as in the block buster *Life is Beautiful*, the insidiousness of which Sander Gilman has recently revealed.[19] Do

sanctimonious sentimentality and optimism in fact indicate noblesse and sensitivity? Are noblesse and optimism meaningful
responses to genocide? Satirists, including Holocaust survivors,
have been suspected of Jewish self-hatred or accused of inciting
anti-Semitic reactions in societies just about to overcome their
anti-Semitic past. Hilsenrath's *Der Nazi und der Friseur* as well
as his later oeuvre elicited outrage among Jews and non-Jews,
problems with publishers, and neo-Nazi demonstrations.[20] At the
same time his works became something like cult-books.

Satirical and grotesque literature conveys the absence of
meaning felt by many survivors and their children. To quote
Beckermann:

> der Tod der Juden . . . hat überhaupt keinen Sinn gehabt.
> Weder die Gründung einer zweiten Republik Österreich
> noch die Gründung eines jüdischen Staates eignen sich
> als Sinngebung des für die Opfer absolut sinnlosen
> Todes in einer Gaskammer in Auschwitz oder Maut-
> hausen.[21]

The proximity of highest cultural and technological achievement
to barbarism causes Hilsenrath and Lind to question the Enlightenment tradition and the process of Jewish Emancipation. They
show the failure of rational thought and suggest that it is impossible to extract meaning from the events of the 1930s and '40s.
Their satires express powerlessness before sadism and cruelty,
they offer no explanation. But they do relieve the reader's frustration through laughter about the absurdity of it all. Thus satire
can bring comfort without pretending to change or save the
world. Hilsenrath and Lind instigate a kind of laughter that im-
plicates the perpetrators—clearly, Jews and Germans react differently to their jokes. The two authors expose greed, the will to
destroy and lack of compassion while carefully avoiding per-
spectives that can be construed as utopian or "constructive."
Their approach gives offense in German-speaking society where
laughter is considered inappropriate in the face of the ultimate
tragedy. Yet they do not configure the Holocaust as a tragedy but
as a man-made obscenity and defy the norms of the dominant
culture by embracing street language as the only way to express
their experience. Through their language and style they proclaim
the bankruptcy of German high culture and the failure of Hu-

manist ideals. In their works there are no admirable characters: no heroic anti-fascist resistance fighters, no brave individualists who go against the grain as does Albrecht Goes's protagonist Margarete Walker in *Das Brandopfer*. By all appearances Goes's narrative, written in 1954, is inspired by noble sentiments and the desire for reconciliation between Gentiles and Jews. Yet the narrator's friendship with Sabine, the daughter of a Gentile mother and a Jewish father—and, according to the Jewish matrilineal tradition not a Jew at all—that symbolizes the new understanding fails to make the point (22). Goes's narrative is imbued with high drama, suggesting that the past is a mystery to be approached with veneration. Concrete steps such as compensation for the victims have no place in this lofty context.

Goes fails in his attempt reconfigure history. Already the term "Wiederherstellung," reestablishing "echte Beziehungen zu Israel," in conjunction with Germany's relationship to Israel gives pause: prior to 1948 Israel did not exist—and why only Israel, if the Nazis murdered Jewish citizens of Germany, Austria, and other European nations? Another problem is the artificiality of saintly Jewish characters, one a rabbi and the other Sabine's father. The oddly patronizing motto of a supposed discussion at the club "Pro Israel," "Redet freundlich mit Jerusalem" (22) encapsulates the cultural bias that pervades the entire text. Despite the plea to remember (22), Goes appears to suggest that the best way to resolve the dilemma of the past is by "einer finsteren Geschichte einiges Licht abgewinnen" (25).

Das Brandopfer tells the story of a woman butcher who was ordered to provide meat for Jewish customers, *meine Juden*, as she refers to them (46). Slowly her shop is transformed into the site of clandestine Shabbat services—Fridays between 5 and 6, the time when Jews do their shopping at the so-called *Judenmetzig*. Margarete Walker also becomes the Jews' secret messenger, and when their deportation is imminent, she hands out generous meat portions. The story culminates in a bomb attack during which Walker is rescued from becoming a "Brandopfer," a sacrifice by fire, by one of her Jewish customers. The flaws in the concept and execution of the story are too numerous to mention. They have been discussed by Ruth Angress [Schickse, form of the Shabbat service, use of the Israeli-Zionist greeting Sha-

lom] and exceed the oversights Goes acknowledges in a dis-
claimer following the 1955 edition.[22]

Goes's glaring ignorance regarding Jewish life reveals a lack
of authorial sincerity. His readers are expected to believe that an
orthodox rabbi would celebrate Shabbes in a Christian butcher
shop under the watchful eye of SS-men while the nearby church
bells ring for the 6 o'clock mass, that an orthodox Jew would say
"Deutsch—gutt, deitsch—nix beese" (44) in the "Tonfall von
Czenstochau" rather than with a Yiddish accent, that he would
defile the Sabbath and Jewish law by accepting non-kosher meat,
and that a German butcher, wife of a Nazi party member, sur-
vives, protected by a Jewish refugee's coat (the owner is mindful
to remove the Yellow Star before he hastens off into the night
and to England). But Frau Walker is branded with a fiery mark
that makes her a good Cain, as it were, a reminder to other Germans. Goes tells all these events without a trace of irony.

Of all the possible stories that could be told about the Holocaust, Goes chose one foregrounding the charity of a Gentile
woman stylized into a martyr. The small risks Frau Walker
takes—after all, her husband is a soldier and a party member—
are incongruous with the bombastic rhetoric. Goes goes to any
length to show that Walker becomes an outsider to German society, ignoring the fact that her Jewish customers are really the
outcasts. Margarete Walker appears extraordinary in every way
but the Jews come across as a pathetic bunch, designed to show-
case German selflessness.

The pattern of Jewish helplessness and Gentile initiative occurs also in later texts, including acclaimed works such as Bruno
Apitz's *Nackt unter Wölfen* and Steven Spielberg's *Schindler's
List*. They, too, cast Jews as passive victims who depend exclu-
sively on Gentile benevolence. Moreover, Goes's "große,
dunkelblonde, helläugige Sabine" (29) is reminiscent of the
racial stereotypes in Artur Dinter's anti-Semitic novels, "der
äußeren Erscheinung nach ganz die Mutter . . dem Wesen nach
der Vater" (29). To the narrator she is "das rätselhafteste
Geschöpf auf der Erde" (29). Only fanatic Nazis come across as
equally one-dimensional. The narrator's sensitivity releases the
reader with the reassuring impression that there are good Gentiles and the saintly Jewish characters appeal to the reader's guilt
and remorse. Critical of the strategic use of postwar philo-

semitism Nadja Seelich in her film *Kieselsteine* (1982) raises the question: "Why do Jews always have to be portrayed as better or worse than other people?"[23] Gentile fiction calls for compassion with Jews if they are of biblical stature and forgiving nature. The foreign-looking customers in Goes's story, referred to as "eine fremde Herde" (44) are far less appealing. The underlying agenda of *Das Brandopfer* is Gentile wish-fulfillment. Goes invented the *Judenmetzig*, a symbol of the mysterious ways in which survivors, former perpetrators and victims, remain forever connected in the spirit of forgiveness in a story palatable to Germans after Auschwitz.

In Bed with the Perpetrator

Close personal interaction and sexual relationships with former perpetrators are a frequent topic in post-Shoah literature. There are marked differences in the portrayal of such relationships depending on the author's background. The novel *Ein Soldat und ein Mädchen* about a sexual encounter between a former Auschwitz SS-guard awaiting execution—inspired by the infamous Irma Grese—and a Jewish Allied soldier was first written by Erich Fried, a refugee from Nazi Austria, in 1946. The work was close to the author's heart, he writes, although or precisely because he had to wrestle with considerable inner resistance because of the issues raised. Published in 1960, the book cuased misunderstandings and controversies in Germany and world-wide.[24] Similarly, Nadja Seelich's film *Kieselsteine*, set in Vienna during the late 1970s, was subject of a debate even while it was still being filmed. Members of the Vienna Jewish community were concerned about possible antisemitic effects the film might have, and non-Jews, including the director Lukas Stepanik, had reservations because of a perceived Jewish bias. *Kieselsteine* deals with the tenuous relationship between the daughter of Holocaust survivors and the son of a Nazi doctor similar in mentality and outlook of the Nazi generation. Bernhard Schlink, born in Germany in 1944, professor of law and a judge in Berlin, thematizes in his 1995 novel *Der Vorleser* an affair between a 15-year old German boy and an older woman, a former concentration camp guard who eventually stands trial in the 1960s.[25] In contrast to the works by the two Jewish authors, Schlink's book

became an international bestseller endorsed even by Oprah Win-
frey.

The three works operate with stereotypes, and they end in
death or near-death. The Nazi characters are blond, and muscu-
lar. Fried's and Schlink's female characters, Helga and Hanna,
are young and sexually attractive.[26] Seelich's Jewish protagonist
Hannah Stern is fascinated by the Nazi son's aggressive body
language and his fascist and racist views alien to her own. In
physical terms, the Nazi son Friedrich Gelpke is unremarkable
and his antics border on the ridiculous. Fried's and Schlink's
Nazi women are cast as objects of male sexual desire as well as
perpetrators, while Seelich's Nazi male represents complete
otherness, the forbidden fruit, to the Jewish woman and she
represents the same to him. The main difference between Schlink
and the two Jewish authors is the level of awareness they attribute to their protagonists, all of whom undergo a maturation process during their confrontation with the Nazi characters. Schlink's
sickly Michael Berg is unaware of Hanna Schmitz's past. In effect, it is possible to read the novel as addressing the issue of
child abuse, easily overread because the victim of the former
Nazi is a boy. Schmitz is to the boy an attractive, experienced
older woman who initiates him into adulthood. The reader, however, cannot but notice that her behavior toward him is precisely
the way she acted around her youthful female love and readers
whom she needed because she herself was illiterate. Before all
this is revealed, the informed reader is already able to speculate
about Schmitz's past and evaluate incongruent behaviors that
baffle the infatuated young man. Fried's soldier who lost family
members and friends in the Holocaust is fully cognizant of the
role of SS-guards in Auschwitz but he takes the risk of an intimate encounter nonetheless. Seelich's Hannah Stern begins to
see Friedrich on a regular basis after a first violently negative reaction to him in order to learn what makes a man like him act the
way he does.

While Schlink devotes a significant part of his book to Frau
Schmitz's and Michael's sexual intimacy and explicit descriptions of the woman's body, the sexual encounter between the
former enemies occupies only a short section of Fried's book. In
Seelich the very last of the emotionally charged encounters between Friedrich and Hannah culminates in his raping her. Fried

is more interested in the psychological and intellectual effects of the Jewish man's night of love with the woman on death row. The love-making itself is described in mystical terms—a complete immersion into the woman's aura and being takes place that erodes the boundaries between victim and perpetrator, Jew and Nazi. The soldier asserts that he loves Helga, that she may not be innocent but she is no longer a criminal either because she has changed after the demise of the system she served (54). Although Nazis drove the soldier's parents to suicide his initial hatred for Helga becomes transformed into a boundless confusing love, the topic of numerous poetic texts attributed to the soldier by a fictional editor. The hatred of Germans dissolves after the night of love and, without his defenses, his erstwhile stable identity disintegrates. When the reader encounters Fried's soldier he is a mental patient writing surrealist stories and poems, a man who has lost his grip on reality as a result of having crossed the boundaries between friend and foe. He holds: "Sogar wenn Helga im Konzentrationslager wirklich ein paar Frauen umgebracht hätte, wer weiß, ob ich ihr nicht auch das noch eher verziehen hätte als zum Beispiel einen schlechten Teint" (226). Fried examines the disturbing questions of change, identity, and emotional complicity that also Hilsenrath addresses when transforming his mass murderer Schultz into an Israeli.

The opposite process takes place in Seelich's *Kieselsteine.* The implicit trust that Nazism no longer poses a danger and that it is impossible for Jews and non-Jews to coexist causes Hannah Stern to associate with an antisemite who never tires to insult and humiliate her. Every episode of *Kieselsteine* reveals the extraordinary degree to which Friedrich is caught up in fascist thinking and emotional patterns and the centrality of Jewish history for Hannah. Flashbacks of her childhood and adolescence help to illustrate the incompatibility of the two individuals. Typically, their meetings end with outrageously insensitive acts committed by Friedrich. The endless debates between Jews and non-Jews, Hannah and Friedrich, invariably end in an impasse and hurt feelings. When Friedrich finally commits the rape it is no surprise to the viewer. Only Hannah's reaction is unexpected: she takes a shower and walks away with a defiant gesture that suggests that the violent act has cured her of her desire for communication with former Nazis and their children. Reconciliation across historical and identity lines, Fried's theme and the starting point of *Kieselsteine,* have become a non-issue. Between Hannah and Friedrich, his friends and hers, reconciliation, let alone understanding is out of the question.

Despite the intensity of the attraction between Schlink's protagonists no long-term relationship is possible because of age barriers and Hanna's past. This is seen as tragic, and the text vindicates the former SS-guard to a point. Incidentally, also Fried exculpates Irma Grese in his afterword, pointing to the testimony of two Hungarian women whose lives she saved (234). Schlink's Hanna turns out to be illiterate and thus not responsible for a report attributed to her. Moreover, she devoted her time in prison to learning to read and inform herself about the Holocaust. In ther words, she does the work of mourning that according to the Mitscherlichs the Germans failed to complete. Eventually she becomes her own executioner by killing herself the day before her release from prison. More subtly a vindication of the Nazi generation also takes place in more subtle terms. The narrator's father is chracterized as an upstanding man, and as he grows older, the narrator criticizes the youthful fervor with which the 60s generation condemned their elders. In many ways the relationship with the SS-woman has a lasting effect on Schlink's protagonist. Having loved and betrayed her causes his inability to form a permanent relationship later on. He is haunted by images of the love—lust and excess—he experienced in the arms of a woman tainted by evil when he was still a minor. A secret allegiance between Hanna and Michael remains as his continued reading for her indicates—she shaped the way he relates to the world and is incapable of breaking the bond that ties him to her.

Back to the Soldiers

In 1995 the Viennese filmmaker and author Ruth Beckermann made a documentary film at the exhibition *Vernichtungskrieg—Verbrechen der Wehrmacht 1941—1944.*[27] Dissatisfied with the tendency of foregrounding the Holocaust victims, Beckermann made the former perpetrators her focus. Her film explores the reactions of World War II veterans who participated in the "war beyond war," the German offensive in Eastern Europe.

Beckermann examines what makes these men so alien to her,[28] how they live with the past, and if anything has changed for them since the 1940s. She also tries to figure out how the victims and their children, including herself, can live among the murderers, and how the murderers can live with themselves and their former victims (85).

The veterans standing before the camera to explain or rationalize their past appear like relics of the past, like the black-and-white photographs and footage of war scenes shown at the exhibit. Beckermann assumes that most of the men who attend the exhibit are haunted by the fear of being found out or want to relive what is in the photos: crimes as well as the soldiers' "joy," "pleasure," and "enthusiasm" (95). She senses that they crave to relive the vitality they felt at the height of their power.

Beckermann omitted interviews that expressed the by now stereotypical denial that has been analyzed *ad nauseum*. Rather, her film shows reactions ranging from defensiveness to remorse, with expressions of uncertainty and ambivalence in between (22). Some of the veterans seem to have had misgivings about their orders even though they followed them anyway. Some reflect critically about their former attitudes. Insightfulness and a total lack of sensitivity often stand side by side. Be it the old men's inability to think analytically, their lack of intellectual curiosity or education, most of them remain caught up in mental habits established in their youth. Some men also display a crude defiance, mental laziness bordering on stupidity.

The majority of the speakers confirm what everyone familiar with Reich, Adorno, Theweleit, and Goldhagen knew all along.[29] Finding new facts, new nuances, new voices is not an easy undertaking. Beckermann's interviewees want to speak about their own suffering and heroism during the bombings in the allied prisoner-of-war camps rather than the Holocaust (19). They lack the imagination to fathom the suffering of their victims. If anything is surprising it is the outrage of some interviewees, including an older woman, at the Nazis. She asserts that the photos at the exhibition surpass everything she suspected and goes on to say that a sense of tragedy has pervaded her life since she learned about the concentration camps (77-78). One may ask: how is it possible as late as 1995 not to know about the atrocities? The Holocaust is the best documented genocide in history. In the debates some veterans admit witnessing crimes—of course without admitting that they took part—others claim they never did. These debates always are dead-end streets. From their ready-made responses—obviously often-repeated lines—it is obvious that many speakers have set modes of speaking about the past. They are shielded against new information that does not conform with their version of the past. Beckermann suspects also that there are codes of silence and solidarity among veterans. Breaking these is tantamount to being a traitor (92).

Beckermann also interviewed women and members of the postwar generations with disappointing results. Over and over the prejudicial attitudes of these innocent bystanders reveal how profoundly they are affected by Nazi ideology. One woman naively uses the term "Jewish Bolshevism" (43), another cites the crimes of Stalinism to exonerate the Wehrmacht (59). A middle-aged woman refuses to accept that the photographs on display are authentic because they threaten her identity by implicating her own relatives in Nazi crimes. "But this here, that makes us believe that our uncles, our fathers, are murderers. Because they represent all of this here as murder, don't they?" A woman exclaims. Her denial is designed to protect her relatives as well as herself: "Aber das hier, das macht uns glauben, daß unsere Onkel, unsere Väter Mörder sind. Denn sie stellen es ja als Mord hin oder nicht? Das kann ich nicht glauben, denn sonst müßte ich mich aufhängen." (71).

Jenseits des Krieges conveys cultural memory from the perspective of a critic/filmmaker who unlike the descendants of the perpetrators has no reason to fear the outcome of her quest. Beckermann is in a position to observe her interviewees' inner conflicts and their denial without the complicity engendered by family loyalty and social conditioning. But she is affected in a different way, as her disbelief shows: "Was sind das für Menschen?" (93) she writes in her film diary, "Was verwirrt sie so?" (95), and "Warum wird ein Mensch so oder so? Warum erzählt er so oder so?" (96). The interviews in *Jenseits des Krieges* suggest that the *Volksgemeinschaft,* the national community, forged by Nazi propaganda, continues to exist, that there are bonds of loyalty that go beyond the generation lines.[30] Most speakers of the older generation derive a positive sense of identity from the larger context of World War II and have successfully transmitted many of their experiences, values, and attitudes to the following generations. As the father- and mother literature by young Germans of the 60s generation showed, there is solidarity with the generation of the fathers and grandfathers, however ambivalent and tense. It is clear, however, that the emotional allegiances with veterans of Hitler's army preclude critical judgment, let alone outright condemnation of the perpetrators. *Jenseits des Krieges* shows Germans and Austrians engaged in the process of forging a cultural memory they can live with, less-than honest versions of the past that offend the Nazi victims and their descendants and threaten the members of the dominant culture in Germany and Austria.

Notes:

[1]Wolfgang Borchert, (Hamburg: Rowohlt, 1988) 37: "Die alten Beckmanns konnten nicht mehr. Hatten sich ein bißchen verausgabt im Dritten Reich, das wissen Sie doch. Was braucht so ein alter Mann noch Uniform zu tragen. Und dann war er ja ein bißchen doll auf die Juden, das wissen Sie doch, Sie, Sohn, Sie. Die Juden konnte Ihr Alter nicht verknusen. Die regten seine Galle an." 37.

[2]Wolfgang Borchert, "Das ist unser Manifest, *Draußen vor der Tür* 112-117. 117. "Denn wir sind Neinsager. Aber wir sagen nicht nein aus Verzweiflung. Unser Nein ist Protest." "Denn wir lieben diese gigantische Wüste, die Deutschland heißt . . . Und um Deutschland wollen wir nicht sterben . . . Um Deutschland wollen wir leben . . . Wir wollen diese Mütter lieben, die Bomben füllen mußten–für ihre Söhne. Wir müssen sie lieben um dieses Leid . . ." (116).

[3]"Für Deutschland. Wir wollen dieses Deutschland lieben wie die Christen ihren Christus: Um sein Leid" (116).

[4]Brigitte Schwaiger, *Lange Abwesenheit* (Hamburg: Rowohlt, 1983).

[5]Rainer-Werner Faßbinder, *Die Ehe der Maria Braun*, Helma Sanders-Brahms, *Deutschland bleiche Mutter*, Peter Handke, *Wunschloses Unglück*, Günter Grass, *Die Bleichtrommel.*

[6]Ilse Aichinger, *Die größere Hoffnung* ; Peter Edel, *Schwester der Nacht* ; Anne Frank, *The Diary of Anne Frank*; Peter Lilienthal, *David* .

[7]Ruth Klüger Angress, "Lanzmann's Shoah and Its Audience." *Contemporary Jewish Writing in Austria,* ed. Dagmar C. G. Lorenz (Lincoln and London: University of Nebraska Press, 1999), 215.

[8]Jean Améry, *Jenseits von Schuld und Sühne: Bewältigungsversuche eines Überwältigten* (Stuttgart: Klett-Cotta, 1997).

[9]Rudolf Hoess, *Commandant of Auschwitz: The Autobiography of Rudolf Hoess* (London: Phoenix, 2000).

[10]Nadja Seelich dir. *Theresienstadt sah aus wie ein Curort.* Wien: extra film 1997.

[11]"The First World War instilled unprecedented hopes for a greater unity between Germans and Jews in many members of the Jewish community of German-speaking Europe. Initial support for the German war effort was nearly unanimous among Jewish liberals, conservatives, and Zionists," writes Noah Isenberg, *Between Redemption and Doom. The Strains of German-Jewish Modernism* (Lincoln and London: University of Nebraska Press, 1999), 54.

[12]Albrecht Goes, *Das Brandopfer* (Frankfurt: S. Fischer, 1985). Original 1954.

[13]Ruth Beckermann, *Unzugehörig* (Wien: Löcker, 1989), 10-11.

[14]Ernestine Schlant, *The Language of Silence. West German Literature and the* Holocaust (New York: Routledge, 1999), 10.

[15]Eric H. Boehm, ed. *We Survived* (New Haven: Yale University Press, 1949).

[16]Edgar Hilsenrath, *Der Nazi und der Friseur* (Frankfurt: Fischer, 1984), 54. Original 1977.

[17]Anat Feinberg, "George Tabori's Mourning Work in *Jubiläum.*" *Staging the Holocaust* (Cambridge: Cambridge University Press, 1998), 267-180. Here: 269.

[18]Gad Kaynar illustrates this in his essay "The Holocaust experience through Theatrical Profanation." *Staging the Holocaust,* 53-69. Here: 56.

[19]Benigni, Roberto, Nicoletta Braschi, Giustino Durano, Horst Buchholz, et al. *Life is Beautiful.* Miramax Home Entertainment; Burbank, Calif. 2000. Sander Gilman, "Is Life Beautiful? Can the Shoah Be Funny? Some Thoughts on Recent and Older Films," *Critical Inquiry* 26/2 (2000), 279-308.

[20]Dagmar C. G. Lorenz, *Verfolgung bis zum Massenmord* (New York: Lang, 1992), 177.

[21]Ruth Beckermann, *Unzugehörig. Österreicher und Juden nach 1945* (Wien: Löcker, 1987), 13. The Auschwitz survivor Jean Améry describes the Holocaust as an enigma, underscoring that monocausal explanations, be they ideological, economic, historical, are doomed to failure. "Weil es nun einerseits nichts wirklich Aufklärendes gibt über die Eruption des radikal Bösen in Deutschland . . . stehen wir alle noch immer vor einem finsteren Rätsel . . . Man weiß: es geschah nicht in einem Entwicklungsland, nicht als direkte Fortsetzung eines tyrannischen Regimes, wie in der Sowjetunion, nicht im blutigen Kampf einer um ihren Bestand bangenden Revolution, wie im Frankreich Robespierres. Es geschah in Deutschland." Jean Améry, *Jenseits von Schuld und Sühne* (Stuttgart: Klett-Cotta, 1980), 9.

[22]Man hat mich aufmerksam gemacht auf einige sachliche Unrichtigkeiten, die mir unterlaufen sind, und eine davon muß hier genannt werden: der Befehl, den "Stern" zu tragen, wurde nicht 1938, sondern erst 1941 erteilt. Man wird es verstehen, wenn ich trotzdem nichts ändere am Text dieser Erzählung, die– ob sie gleich auf freier Erfinding beruht–niemand eine "frei erfundene" Geschichte nennen wird, eher ließ sich von "gebundener Erfindung" sprechen (75).

[23]Nadja Seelich, *Kieselsteine.* Dir. Lukas Stepanik. Cinéart, Filmverleih

Hans Peter Hofmann, 1982.

[24]Erich Fried, *Ein Soldat und ein Mädchen* (Frankfurt: Fischer, 1960), 230; 233.

[25]Bernhard Schlink, *Der Vorleser* (Zürich: Diogenes, 1995).

[26]Fried 20: "Zu erwähnen ist noch Helgas Schönheit, die von Anfang an bis zum Ende die Berichterstatter und Pressephotographen auf sie aufmerksam gemacht und die Vertreter der Justiz–lauter Männer–fast ein wenig erbittert hatte, soweit diese sich Gefühlen nicht versperrten."

[27]Hamburger Institut für Sozialforschung ed. *Vernichtungskrieg. Verbrechen der Wehrmacht 1941 bis 1944. Ausstellungskatalog* (Hamburg: Institut für Sozialforschung, 1996). In conjunction with this catalogue see also the interviews in Hamburger Institut für Sozialforschung, ed. *Besucher einer Ausstellung. Die Ausstellung "Vernichtungskrieg. Verbrechen der Wehrmacht 1941-1944" in Interview und Gespräch,* and Hamburger Institut für Sozialforschung, ed. *Eine Ausstellung und ihre Folgen. Zur Rezeption der Ausstellung "Vernichtungskrieg. Verbrechen der Wehrmacht 1941 bis 1944"* (Hamburg: Institut für Sozialforschung, 1997). On the topic of the German military and prisoners of war see: Reinhard Otto, *Wehrmacht, Gestapo und sowjetische Kriegsgefangene im deutschen Reichsgebiet 1941/42* (München: Oldenbourg, 1998).

[28]Robert Mernasse writes in "Sterbensworte." *Jenseits des Krieges,* 9-16: "Noch nie in der Geschichte hat sich durch so hartnäckiges Schweigen so viel unverbrüchliches Wissen akkumuliert."

[29]Hannah Arendt, *Eichmann in Jerusalem* (München: Piper, 1964).

[30]Eduard von Borsody dir. *Wunschkonzert.* Indianapolis, Ind.: International Historic Films; 1984; Veit Harlan dir. *Jud Süss.* Chicago: IHF Productions, 1988; Fritz Hippler dir. *Der ewige Jude.* Tamarelle International Films 1986; Leni Riefenstahl dir. *Triumph des Willens.* Chatsworth, CA : Timeless Video, 1996.

Torn Between Love, Hate, and Guilt: "I Hate this Language which I Love"

Lisa Kahn

Introduction

The thirteenth annual Harry H. Kahn Memorial Lecture occurred on April 15, 2002, and we were excited to bring Prof. Lisa Kahn from Texas Southern University back to our campus. She had honored us some years ago with a memorable reading from her poetry. As a scholar and poet she has played a major role in the German literary scene in the Unitd States and abroad.

It is with great pleasure and excitement that I welcome our distinguished guest and good friend Prof. Lisa Kahn (née Kupfer) back to our campus this afternoon. Some of us will remember her visit to the University of Vermont in the fall of 1988 at which time she did a most memorable reading from her poetry. In fact, let me remind all of you that she will once again read from her poetry for us tomorrow in the Phi Beta Kappa room. It is indeed an honor to have Lisa Kahn bless us with two performances during her visit to Vermont.

Prof. Kahn was born in Berlin, attended school in Leipzig, and received her Ph.D. from the University of Heidelberg in 1953. Her late husband Robert L. Kahn had also moved to Leipzig from Nuremberg in the mid-thirties, but Lisa and Robert Kahn did not meet until she came to the United States on an early Fulbright scholarship to study at the University of Washington at Seattle during the academic year 1950-1951. Robert Kahn had escaped Nazi Germany, having lost his parents in the horrors of the Holocaust. Together the Kahns built a new life in the New World with their children Peter and Beatrice. Both of them became professors of German as well as acknowledged poets, and Lisa Kahn will in fact speak to us about the life and fate of her former husband Robert Kahn as a Holocaust survivor in

the United States. Doubtlessly you will be very interested in
Robert Kahn after this lecture, and I would like to draw your attention to his book of poetry entitled *Tonlose Lieder* (1978) that
his wife published after his death in 1970. There is also a very
comprehensive study by Klaus Beckschulte in German entitled
"ich hasse die sprache, die ich liebe": *Das Leben und Werk von
Robert Ludwig Kahn* (1996).

In 1962 the Kahn family moved to Houston, where Robert
Kahn advanced his career in German literature as a renowned
scholar of Romanticism and chairperson of the Department of
German at Rice University. In 1968 Lisa Kahn, who had dedicated her life until then to the well-being of her family while
working as a teacher of German and French, started upon her
own career as a distinguished professor of German at Texas
Southern University in Houston. After being widowed in 1970,
Lisa Kahn forged ahead as a scholar and poet with her characteristic enthusiasm and energy. Her work has been supported by
Fulbright, National Endowment of the Humanities, Alexander
von Humboldt, and Goethe Institute grants. She has been guest
professor at the University of St. Thomas (Houston), she served
as chairperson of the Foreign Language Department at Texas
Southern University, she became vice president of the Texas
chapter of the American Association of Teachers of German, and
she was president of the Houston Area Teachers of Foreign Languages. Clearly Lisa Kahn has dedicated much of her professional life to the teaching of German language, culture, and literature. It is no surprise then that she received the Ehrenstern
Award for her exceptional dedication and outstanding achieve-
ments in furthering the German Heritage in Texas.

In recognition of her creative work as an accomplished literary author, Lisa Kahn was elected as a member of International
PEN in 1982 in London. She became a member of the American
PEN in 1985, followed by a membership in the Austrian PEN in
1989. In 1990 she received the "Bundesverdienstkreuz 1. Klasse
der Bundesrepublik Deutschland," one of the highest honors that
anybody can receive from the government of the Federal Republic of Germany. More recently she was also honored with the
Pegasus Award from the Poetry in the Arts Association (Austin,
Texas), and she was named Poeta Laureata at the University of
New Mexico in Albuquerque, New Mexico.

A glance at her numerous scholarly publications shows the depth and breadth of Lisa Kahn's interests and work. There are papers on language instruction, on cultural questions, and on such modern authors as Kurt Tucholsky, Günter Kunert, Irmtraud Morgner, Friederike Mayröcker, Ernst Jandl, and others. Her commitment to social issues can be seen from an early paper entitled "The Industrial Proletariat as Portrayed in Literature and Art from 1844 to 1932," *Texas Southern University Faculty Research Journal*, 1 (1976), 74-84. Already in the late seventies, when it was by no means fashionable in German studies to pay special attention to women's issues, Lisa Kahn published a seminal paper on "Contemporary German-American Women Authors: A Survey," *Schatzkammer*, 4 (1978), 53-65, that was followed by other such publications, the most important being "Kontemporäre deutschsprachige Literatur in den USA," in: Heinz Kloss (ed.), *Deutsch als Muttersprache in den Vereinigten Staaten* (1985), 155-169. As a scholar and as a poet, Lisa Kahn is very much aware of the fact that she stands between two languages and two cultures. This can be seen from such insightful essays as "'Amerika: Land der beschränkten Möglichkeiten': Deutschsprachige Autoren in den Vereinigten Staaten von Amerika 1938-1983," *Zeitschrift für Kulturaustausch*, 38 (1988), 206-217; "Why Write Poetry? Why in German? For Whom?" *Max Kade Occasional Papers in German-American Studies*, no. 5 (2001), 1-16; and her extremely influential anthologies *Reisegepäck Sprache* (1979), *In Her Mother's Tongue* (1983, with Jerry Glenn), and *Deutschschreibende Autoren in Nordamerika* (1990). Since 1992 Lisa Kahn has also been a most influential member of the editorial board of *Trans-Lit: Journal of the Society for Contemporary American Literature in German*. In this regard I am happy to report that a number of our students have published their poems and short prose in this journal with the help of Lisa Kahn. In fact, our former graduate student Folke-Christine Moeller-Sahling, herself an Assistant Professor of German by now, wrote her M.A. thesis here in our Department of German and Russian on *Lisa Kahn: Eine deutschschreibende Schriftstellerin in den USA* (1995)

Her own poetry and prose have appeared in Austria, Germany, Switzerland, Canada, and the United States in journals, magazines, and anthologies. Some of her eighteen books include *Klopfet an, so wird Euch nicht aufgetan* (1975), *Feuersteine* (1978), *David am Computer und andere Gedichte* (1982), *From My Texan Log Cabin* (1984), *Bäume* (1984), *Wer mehr liebt. Kurzgeschichten und Märchen* ('984), *Tor und Tür* (1986), *Kinderwinter* (1986), *Kreta, fruchtbar und anmutsvoll* (1988), *Today I Commanded the Wind / Heute befahl ich dem Wind* (1994), *Kälbchengeschichten* (1997), *Flussbettworte / Fluvial Discourse* (1998), *The Calf Who Fell in Love with a Wolf* (1999), and *The Bluebonnet Trail of Verses* (2002). Her poetry and short prose touch on many aspects of life, both in a serious and thoughtful as well as light and humorous fashion. There are texts for children and adults dealing with joy and sadness, with separation, death, and the Holocaust, with Germany and America, with culture and language, with nature and technology, and above all with love and understanding in a world riddled by atrocities, terror, and war. In this darkness Lisa Kahn's work represents a warm ray of hope. As the title of her poetry volume *Atlantische Brücke* (1992) implies, Lisa Kahn sees herself as a bridge builder between the German speaking world and the United States in particular and among humans in general. Of course, she also has continued her husband Robert Kahn's desire of building solid bridges between the Jewish and German people. As we remember our dear friend Harry H. Kahn today, let us do the same for Robert L. Kahn, and let us applaud Lisa Kahn for her courageous and humane scholarly and poetic work for a better world based on understanding and love.

Lecture

When Professor Wolfgang Mieder from the University of Vermont invited me to deliver a presentation at the annual Harry H. Kahn Memorial Lecture Series, I was rather overwhelmed by this honor. At the same time, I hesitated, realizing immediately that I would have to speak about the fate of my husband Robert L. Kahn – no relation to the Harry H. Kahn family. Though my husband died in 1970, 32 years ago, the circumstances of his death still make it difficult for me to remember and to talk publicly about them.

My husband was born in Germany. He was Jewish. He was persecuted. He was also a Germanist, a professor of German, and a writer who had published interesting work. Had I spoken about him 40 or 30 years ago, a number of people in the audience might have known him personally, or of him. So I decided to accept Professor Mieder's kind invitation to speak of him today, when very few people remember him, and hope that I can revive the memory of him.

Before I start to tell you about Robert's life, I would like to quote a woman who survived the Holocaust: "If you lost your parents in a concentration camp, you can never be truly happy again."[1] Perhaps, this is a generalization, but it was, despite moments, hours, even days of great happiness, true for Robert L. Kahn.

After I had written these introductory remarks, my son suggested a quote from his father as a title, namely: "Ich hasse diese Sprache, die ich liebe" (I hate this language which I love). I thought however, that the feelings of guilt that weighed so heavily on Robert should also be mentioned in the title.

Since my husband was a poet, I believe it very appropriate to start with a poem by a famous Holocaust writer, Primo Levi:

Shemà

You who live secure
In your warm houses,
Who return at evening to find
Hot food and friendly faces:

Consider whether this is a man,
Who labors in the mud
Who knows no peace
Who fights for a crust of bread
Who dies at a yes or a no
Consider whether this is a woman,
Without hair or name
With no more strength to remember

Eyes empty and womb cold
As a frog in winter.

Consider that this has been:
I commend these words to you.
Engrave them on your hearts
When you are in your house
When you walk on your way,
When you go to bed, when you rise.
Repeat them to your children.
Or may your house crumble,
Disease render you powerless,
Your offspring avert their faces from you.[2]

The *Shema* is *Act I* of the service (it is the same in every Jewish congregation in America.)

Schema Ysrael! Hear oh Israel, Adonai is our God, Adonai is *one*. The sages called it "kabbala ol shamayim" (the acceptance of the yoke of heaven). It is the center statement of the Jewish faith. It bonds the person who prays with God. Pious Jews should say it twice, in the morning and in the evening. Primo Levi changes this most important and positive prayer into a powerful lament and accusation of the utmost proportion and strength.

Since Kahn's lyrical work consistently reflects his experiences, it is essential to realize the traumatic experiences of his childhood and youth. Ludwig Robert Kahn was born in 1923 into an affluent business family, which traced its ancestry to Tann i. d. Rhön. He was the second child, after a sister who was born in 1920. Apparently the Kahn family felt well accepted and at home in Nürnberg. Robert's mother, Beatrice, was musical, giving recitals of "Lieder" by Schubert, Brahms, etc. in the circle of their friends. Gustav, his father, was a businessman, marketing metals, old and new. Robert's sister went to a public school, but Robert went to the Jewish Carlebach-School. Though Robert did not know about it, it is interesting that in 1924, one year after his birth, the first pogrom took place on the Jewish cemetery in Nürnberg.[3]

As is known, Nürnberg became the "Stadt der Reichsparteitage." The climate turned "braun" sooner than in any other city. The synagogue, which the family attended, was destroyed during "Kristallnacht," but the Kahns had already left by then. By 1937 more than half the Jewish population had emigrated.

The Kahns moved to Leipzig in 1935,[4] the largest city in Sachsen, often referred to as "das rote Sachsen." The family chose Leipzig, because Beatrice's only brother, Dr. Joseph Freudenthal, lived there. Of course, the anti-Semitic atmosphere caught soon up with them[5] in Leipzig, and the social downward spiral continued.

Robert's father was no longer an entrepreneur with car and chauffeur, but a small employee. They had to live in a small apartment, even smaller now that they had taken Beatrice's mother in. Yet Robert, now 12 years old, still went to a Hebrew school. Once in a while the family even attended a concert in the Gewandhaus where the monument of its first conductor, Felix Mendelssohn, stood in front of the building. To attend "Gewandhauskonzerte" was quite typical for the Jewish "Bildungsbürgertum." However, at these occasions, the family was always afraid that someone might identify them as Jews.[6] It was of utmost importance to the parents that the children would be protected. Robert's maternal uncle, Joseph Freudenthal, had emigrated to New York, and in 1938, shortly before Kristallnacht, the parents were able to send Robert's sister, Susan, to join him in New York. She survived the farewell and separation from the family because she was already 18 years old. Her family in New York took her into their home and helped her to get a job. Also, she exchanged letters with her parents. Robert's uncle, Josef, was supposed to pay for Robert's emigration and voyage, but he was not able to do so.

In November of 1938, during Kristallnacht, Robert's father, Gustav Kahn, was arrested and brought to Sachsenhausen. When he was released, he was a broken man, physically and especially spiritually. At this point, I would like to read one of Robert Kahn's poems from his lyrical volume "tonlose lieder" ("soundless songs"). The poem "empfindsame ballade" is the only poem about his father.[7] While Gustav Kahn was in Sachsenhausen, Beatrice, Robert, and the grandmother had, of course, no income. They found refuge in the Jewish Home for the Aged in Leipzig.

At the time Robert's father was released and returned from Sachsenhausen, it was of utmost concern to find some way to rescue Robert. On the 10th of May 1939, a few days after Robert's 16th birthday, he was sent with a Kindertransport, via Bentheim in Holland, to Harwich in England.[8] Since he was one of the oldest children, he went to school only for a brief time. Then he fell, so to speak, through the protective net that was available for younger children, who were placed in families. He was considered an "Enemy Alien," shipped to the Isle of Man, there to await transportation to Canada as POWs (Prisoners of War). Thus, the life-threatening situation for this boy never seemed to end.

He would say with Job:

> Warum hast du mich dir zur Zielscheibe gemacht? (Why did you make me your target?)

> Warum bin ich dir zur Last geworden? (Why did I become a burden to you?)[9]

And there would never be an answer.

Most children see their mother as their primary relationship. In cases where there is no mother, those who survive almost always develop a feeling of guilt, that they survived "undeservedly," in comparison to the mother! These children are prone to suffer from depression, and frequently a depression so deep that there is no other way out but to end their own lives.[10]

The security, which the parents had desired for him in England, did not materialize. The most imminent danger was, of course, that a German submarine might torpedo them when crossing the Atlantic to Canada. This actually happened with the "Andora Star," a POW ship that had left two weeks before. It was hit, everybody on board perished. Later, after protests in the British press and in Parliament, these transatlantic transports were stopped.

Robert was now an enemy alien in a Canadian POW camp, together with men of all ages and all persuasions, including Nazis. The POW camp was located on the Ile aux Noix in the Richelieu River in Quebec. Apparently, a fort had already existed there, built during the French-Indian wars. Though the Canadian guards never mistreated them, life was, of course, far from pleasant, particularly due to the icy winters.

At this time, his faith, which he had accepted as a matter of fact in his upbringing, started to become somewhat porous. It was not yet crumbling, but he wondered, "And the sky was naked, and empty, all the heavens and God were hiding their face." (Rejsl Zychlinski)[11]

However, the Canadian Red Cross apparently checked once a month to see whether the POWs had enough blankets, and soon Jewish auxiliary organizations tried to help with food, encouraging letters and even an occasional visit. Some of the older POWs organized classes for the young, persecuted boys, who longed for their parents and their families. They began just a few weeks after they had started their imprisonment in the camp. This was by far the best medicine for them. Among these older POWs were lawyers, teachers, scientists and many other professionals. They set up a regular classroom curriculum with a wide range of classes, including math, English, history, Latin, geography, chemistry, and physics. At the end of the war, when the young people had to take their graduation examinations, all the boys passed, and the Canadian Government recognized their matriculation as official. In other words, they could enter colleges and universities.

Robert regularly received letters from his sister in Cincinnati and family members in New York, but he did not receive any news from Germany. Gustav Kahn, his father, had taken sleeping pills the night before two of his sisters were to be transported to a concentration camp. Robert did not know about it until 1945, nor did he learn, until after the war, of his mother's demise in 1942 in Auschwitz.

Of course, he was constantly worried about his parents, and without the demands of the daily classes in camp and the friendships which developed among the Jewish POWs, he might never have survived.

It was at this time that Robert changed his name from Ludwig Robert to Robert Ludwig. He did not want to be named after a Bavarian king, though, of course, Ludwig I. had been dead for more than 100 years.

During his internment, a couple from Halifax, with three married daughters, started corresponding with Robert. After the war, they took him into their home, and he worked in their stores, but soon decided that he wanted to go to Dalhousie University in Halifax.

In his classes at the camp he had shown great interest in German literature, perhaps because he was already familiar with some of Goethe, Lessing, and Heine from his home and high school in Germany. He also established an interest in philosophy which later led him to Spinoza and still farther away from his religious background. The final break with religion occurred when he learned of his mother's death. He said many times to himself, to me, and to whoever would listen: "If God is supposed to be omniscient, omnipotent, and benevolent, he could not have permitted the Holocaust. There is no equation possible. One of the characteristics is missing. And why should I believe in such a figure lacking in knowledge, power, or goodness?"

Though an agnostic, he still was interested in Jewish affairs. We lit candles every Friday night, also when we had Non-Jewish friends as dinner guests on Fridays. We celebrated Chanucka; were invited to annual Seders at various friends' houses. He also took a great interest in Israel, realizing how important it was that there was one state in the world, no matter how small, where Jews could feel safe. At the same time he felt guilty that he had survived while the person whom he loved most and who was the best possible person in the world for him, his mother, had to perish in Auschwitz. He was never able to overcome this feeling of guilt. Memories of her superior character, her never-ending love for him, her kindness and goodness of heart would never leave him. He carried them with him for over a quarter of a century, and wanting to be close to her was certainly an influential factor in the decision to end his life.

Joseph Hahn, in his deeply moving book *Eklipse und Strahl*,[12] speaks of "Verhängnis und Sühne, ein jähes Geweh, stößt deiner Mutter Anflug ans Ohr"[13] in his poem "Im Winter," i.e. fate and entonement, a sudden anguish pushes your mother's approach to your ear."[14]

Robert once recited the poem "Meine Mutter" by Else Lasker-Schüler to me, which translates:

My Mother

The candle burns on my table
for my mother
all night long
for my mother

My heart burns under the shoulder blade
all night long
for my mother[15]

Permit me to add a translation of Robert's poem

lied von zwei toten Müttern

Yesterday i dreamed of my mother
she was wearing a white dress
she smiled peacefully and cheerful
i am glad
always in my dreams i see my mother
naked and pale
she trembles on the cold cement floor
in her hand she holds a towel
i suffocate with hatred[16]

Robert presents two sides of his mother when he considers the contrast between the two pictures of the mothers, and he suffocates with hatred for those who committed the crime.

This longing for his mother, sometimes hidden, often rising to the surface, was always intense. There are so many possibilities to feel this longing, but the worst kind of longing is not the one for somebody who left not to return, but somebody who is dead and will never return. And this longing can grow like a cancer. There just is no remedy for it, no medication, no passing of time, and sometimes there even is no reason for this longing any more. But longing does not need any reason.

Robert once told me that as a child he never wanted to go to bed. There is a Yiddish tale about an angel of sleep who told the children stories so that they fell asleep, but the three brothers *If, Had I, Would I* always woke the child up again. The angel of sleep puts us to sleep, but the brothers *If, Had I, Would I* always wake us up again, dance with their questions around us and pre-

vent us from falling asleep again.—How does one overcome this
intense trauma?

When he left Germany with the Kindertransport, he never
said a final goodbye to his parents, because the idea was to re-
unite once the war would be over. He had always hoped that his
parents would survive. There is no recipe for dealing with such
tragedy. And even in those years in which he tried to manage a
"normal" life, he still had hope. When he learned the truth in
1945, he was devastated. An old cliché says, "time heals all
wounds." That's a myth. Robert tried to go on, to build a new
life. But the wounds did not heal.

The family in Halifax was well off and took Robert into their
house and hearts. They had no heir for their department stores in
Quebec. Robert helped in the businesses but was also allowed to
go to College. He attended Dalhousie University where he received his magister artium in history. However, these years were
not happy ones. He had to disappoint the expectations and hopes
of his "Canadian parents" by refusing to take over their business
and become their adopted son. He went to McGill, and later to
Toronto, where he obtained his Ph.D. in German under Böschen-
stein. The relationship to Halifax naturally turned cooler, but
they visited us once when we lived in Seattle where we spent
some of our happiest years.

The price he paid for having survived, however, was the
guilt-feelings that he should not have survived. It was, to speak
again with Primo Levi in his "Crow's Song," always the same
sad news:

I flew without resting,
A hundred miles without resting,
To find your window,
To find your ear,
To bring you the sad tidings
That rob you of sleep's joy,
That taint your bread and wine,
Lodge every evening in your heart.[17]

Robert started his professional career as an instructor at the
University of Washington in Seattle, and soon was promoted to
Assistant Professor in German. Many people have wondered
why of all subjects he chose to teach the language of a country

that had wounded him so much, why he did not stay with history or philosophy. I asked him this question myself, shortly after I met him in Seattle at the University of Washington. And he would respond, "it is not the language, which has hurt me, and certainly not its literature."

He and I had a lot in common, not just language and love for literature. I majored at that time in psychology. Erwin Chargaff, about whom our colleague and friend Professor Mieder has written in detail, describing the use of proverbs and aphorisms, said "Die Zeit hörte auf, alle Wunden zu heilen."[18] How true. But it seemed that these wounds hurt less. Chargaff, whose mother was taken in 1943 from Vienna to Auschwitz, says: "Ich habe viel über ihren Tod nachgedacht, und Nachdenken hilft nicht viel."[19]

Alfred Kubin caught the demons, night ghosts and nightmares, which overwhelmed him, in his paintings and hundreds of drawings.

And this is how Robert arrived at the formulation: "ich hasse diese Sprache, die ich liebe." He could have never said: "ich hasse dieses Land, das ich liebe," because he did not love the country – there were so many aspects of the "land" that were unpleasant, sometimes even threatening to him, though, of course, there were also times when he enjoyed the landscape, the art, music, and travel. The question which other emigrants may have had about German language and literature, Brecht, Hans Sahl, Stefan Zweig, Peter Heller, Harry Zohn, Erich Fried, and especially Joseph Roth, to name just a few, never existed in his mind.[20]

As you know, Robert was not the only teacher of German who happened to be Jewish. You have had a number of them here as speakers for the Holocaust series. Robert's publications clearly show how his interest moved from social concerns to historical events, linguistic evaluations, creative interpretations, and finally, his own creative work.

He participated in the research for the George Forster *Gesamtausgabe* (*Streitschriften und Fragmente zur Weltreise*, Vol. I-IV) with Gerhard Steiner, University of Berlin -- at that time still "East" Berlin – the Humboldt University, as well as for the Friedrich Schlegel *Gesamtausgabe* with Ernst Behler. (The work on Schlegel led to essays about Caroline[21] and especially

Novalis,[22] who interested him the most during the year before his death and the year of his death, and about whom he had already published an article.)

Of those German and Austrian Jewish professors who came as emigrants to the United States, some had already established themselves as teachers, writers, and poets, before they came to the United States, but some were refugees like Robert. They had suffered similar fates, but to my knowledge, none of them had lost their mother in a death camp. His immense love for her was complemented by his interest in and love for literature, music, teaching, language, poetry, nouns which are all feminine in German: Die Literatur, die Poesie, die Sprache, die Musik. All of these were in a confluence with his remembering his mother, and his identifying these areas with her and the memory of her.

And he wrote everything in German. A famous Polish poet, Szeslaw Milosz who was persecuted in Russia but later able to emigrate to the United States (he won the Nobel Prize for Literatur in 1980), wrote a poem about his mother tongue, which I would like to share with you in parts. It is called "My Faithful Language." Robert Kahn could have written it.

My Faithful Language

My faithful language
I served you
every night I would put little pots with color in front of you
so that you would have the birch tree, the cricket and the bull-finch
which dwell in my memory.

That lasted for many years
you were my native land, because I missed it
I thought you might also be the mediator
between the good people and me
even if there were only twenty, ten
or some yet unborn.

Now I confess to my doubts
There are moments when it seems to me my life has been spent,

for you are the language of the undignified
the language of the unreasonable and of those who hate.

But who would I be without you?

My faithful language
perhaps it is I who should save you after all
So I shall continue
to put little vessels with paint in front of you
with light and clean colors, if possible,
because some kind of order and beauty in this disarray is
needed.[23]

So there was this great love for his mother, for his happy childhood memories in a closely-knit family, for the language and especially German literature, Goethe, Lessing, but not just the clas-
sics, also Heine, the Romantics (Schlegel, Novalis), and contemporary literature. He wrote an essay on Hans Carossa and translated a poem by Nelly Sachs with an interpretation.

He invited Siegfried Lenz, Ilse Aichinger, Hilde Domin,
Horst Bienek, to name just a few of the annual speakers, to give
readings at the university, and later we had them as guests at our
home. Others we met when we were invited to their readings at
the University of Texas in Austin, e.g., Günter Kunert, Horst
Bienek, Max Frisch and others. I am certain, that a number of
these visitors inspired him to continue to write himself.

Robert was also ambitious. In his early forties, he was the
Department Chairman at a well-renowned university. He was
also rightly proud. However, tensions existed between his love
for family and German literature on one hand, and his hatred and
contempt for the Nazi régime and the Nazi years in Germany,
which robbed him of his family, pushed him into poverty and
imprisoned him in a POW camp. This tension never died. The
death of his parents battled the positive memories of his childhood.

It is quite interesting that in one of his poems from that time
"prophetic I" he describes the landscape and says:

Stretching before me
the golden land
the green forests

clean farms
the blue smoke
driving onto the fields
slowly....[24]

and he continues with the description of this farmland. When I
read this poem for the first time, I had expected that the "golden
land" would be Israel and was surprised to learn that he was describing some German village.

Writing poetry was probably one avenue open to him
through which he might overcome the past, but as Friedrich Torberg confessed "wo ich auch gehe, flattern die dunklen Ge-
wänder der Toten um mich" (wherever I walk, the dark robes of
the dead fly around me).

But there occurred a ritardando. It seemed that at times life
was worthwhile after all. Our children were born in 1953 and
1959. In 1961, Robert received an Alexander von Humboldt
grant to spend one year in Marbach. He was filled with pride. He
had no fear of putting his foot on German soil. Since Marbach
did not have any living accommodations for a family of four for
just one year, we rented an apartment in Stuttgart, a city we all
found quite attractive. As it turned out, our "Wohnung" was in
walking distance to the apartment of a woman who was also a
Jewish refugee who had permanently returned from her refuge in
Sweden as Professor of Philosophy to the Technische University
in Stuttgart, Käte Hamburger. The similarities of their fate made
for a warm relationship despite their difference in age. There was
a unique understanding of each other. She was also an agnostic,
an admirer of Spinoza, so they had much in common. Helmut
Kreuzer,[25] then a young instructor at the Technical University in
Stuttgart, and his wife, the writer and poet Angelika Jakob, also
became close friends. Käte Hamburger introduced Bob to other
faculty. We also traveled, going to France and Spain, to Nürnberg, where we saw the house where he was born, Dietzstr.1,
which had been occupied by a Nazi big-wig after the Kahns left
for Leipzig. Then we went to Greece. During that visit Robert
did not feel dejected, nervous, depressed. It seemed as if he had
been able to banish the shadows and pain of the Holocaust. He
met other former Jewish emigrants, even a couple from Israel.

While in Stuttgart, Robert received an invitation to fly to Houston for an interview at Rice University. He accepted their offer, and after the return from Stuttgart in the fall of 1963 to the United States, we moved from Seattle to Houston. In 1964, he became chairman of the German Department. In 1967, he received a 3-months stipend to do research on Lichtenberg, which we spent in Göttingen. Both our children were bilingual.

But the happiness would not last after our return to Houston from Göttingen. He had good friends at Rice; he was popular with his students, especially his graduate students, some of whom are still in contact with me. Apparently his seemingly happy demeanor was only a thin veneer, easily destroyed again. Two developments robbed him of his new-found self-esteem and peace and introduced new feelings of insecurity in one area, hate and despair in another one.

What might still have become an idyllic life was now attacked, degraded, and later completely destroyed. The price he paid for having survived the Holocaust turned again into the guilt feeling that he should not have survived, since his mother had not survived. To die was the only way out for him in his dilemma. Which were the two developments that led to the catastrophe?

Robert had started to write poetry. Rose Ausländer in a poem says:

My Nightingale

Once upon a time
my mother was a doe
the golden brown eyes
the poverty
stayed with her from the doe period

Here she was
half angel, half human
the cove was mother
when I asked her
what she would have liked to become
she said: a nightingale

Now she is a nightingale
half angel, half human
night after night I listen to her
in the garden of my sleepless dreams ..."[26]

And Robert, whose English was impeccable (after all, he had left Germany when he was fifteen), started to write his poetry in German.

"Heimat ist für diese Dichter nicht mehr die ursprüngliche Geburtsstadt, wo sie mißbraucht, verfolgt, und schließlich vertrieben wurden. Sie fliehen in die Heimat der Sprache, in Lyrik und Prosa, Sprache ist Ersatz für Heimatsverlust." ("Heimat" is no longer the place of their birth, where they were abused, persecuted, and expelled. They escape into the language of the "Heimat" or the "Heimat" of their language, into lyrics, into prose. Language is the "Ersatz" for the loss of one's home.) As Muriel Ruckeyser states: "A poem invites you to feel. More than that: it invites you to respond. And better than that, a poem invites a total response. This response is total, but it is reached through the emotions. A fine poem will seize your imagination intellectually – but the way is through emotion."[27] Rilke talked about the "Beheimatung in der Heimatlosigkeit"; this might be contrasted with the fact that the personal satisfaction for this experience was not open for Robert. It remained closed.

Audrey Lorde, the American poet, says: "Poetry is not a luxury ... it is a bridge across our fears ... sends an essential message – poetry is everyone's legacy ... and it is central to the human spirit."[28]

Virginia Wolfe demands to have a room of one's own. Important as it might have been for her as a woman, this was and is, of course, not always possible for the writer. But language for a bilingual person, can become such a place of one's own, a hiding place, an intimate sphere where the writer can unfold his/her creativity. For most of us who live in a country whose language is not the first one we learned, we must dig deeper to find our roots, which nourish us when we write creative prose or poetry. It provides warmth and security, and there are also metaphors which we use to express our connectedness to both languages, such as "Sprachbrücke": we bridge the New and the Old World. There are forces in nature which help us with the bridge-building, wind, water, even stones, and of course memories, and even death which allows life and evolution to continue in other forms.

Adorno's slogan that it is impossible to write poetry after the Holocaust was soon invalidated, as many writers and poets started to reflect the Holocaust in their work. Chalom Ben Chorin, born in Nürnberg, living since 1935 in Jerusalem, says: "you can emigrate from a country, but not from your mother's tongue. The inseparable ties with the language is for the writer whose instrument remains the language, even more intensive than it is for other people."[29]

Even if we have learned the language of another country, which became our home to a certain perfection, the language of the soul, the language of the unconscious, the dream, remains the mother tongue.[30] "Sie (die Muttersprache) steht über den Schwenkungen alles Politischen, über jeder Ideologie."[31]

When Robert started to write poetry after returning from Göttingen in 1967, it seemed as if this writing which, of course, was in German would be a kind of therapy for him. I was very glad that he found this outlet, and everything might have turned out for the better had he not planned to publish his poetry. In the sixties in Germany nobody was interested in lyrics by a German emigrant. Germans were pre-occupied with their post-war "Aufbau," with the novelists Grass, Böll, Lenz and Frisch. So when he sent his poems to the publishing houses in Germany, they were politely rejected. He called them "Tonlose Lieder." Permit me to read some of them, in translation, to you. Of course, the original poems were in German.

pontus 1

don't hold it against me
i have remained faithful
to her

the small puddles
of memory
drops of oil
flowing on smooth
darkness
no mirror of any
gloomy hours

just some times
there is a glimmer
of turquoise
only for a second
bluish-gray yellow-green
fading away

my father's house
the sounds of fleeting steps
the mood of light wings

quickly fading
the warmth of
hand and cool
lips

forgotten dreams
of a pale race
burning sun traces
in the desert
blue and white temples
crosses distorted by a moon
lamb sacrifice wind
burnt cedars
jehova's rage his
blessing flight and
hunt his word
is to believe to meditate
betrayed secretive
melodies of jerusalem
decayed walls

salty-red waves
of the mediterranean
a slave market
raped hung

rules once explained
never again obeyed
prayers hurried songs
unrestrained and wild

they pass leaving no trace
disgraced without arms
on castilian dusty
roads barren
hills wine
grows around
worms from
the roots of my
race a branch of priests
traces in the desert there's
where my people rest

don't blame me
i have remained faithful
to her
(this also is true:
i hate this language
which I love)[32]

In the epilogue to the partial reprint of Robert's book in 1986, Käte Hamburger stresses that this title is not a mere oxymoron. She says: "Wordless songs are, of course, possible, but voiceless songs negate the concept of 'song,' they can only exist when the sound is suffocated. The voice remains in the throat. It is the voice of a bitter cynicism, born out of suffering, at times reminiscent of Heine who could not have fathomed the unimaginable experiences of our country. The deathly horrors of these 'timely' poems are written from a subjective existential experience. The lyric form of these poems is most adequate. They are temporary poetry in its most profound sense."[33]

Robert's frustration and overwhelming disappointment that his poetry remained unpublished – and he sent it to all the known, and a number of unknown German literary magazines and publishing houses -- hurt him deeply. They were not returned with slips, because, after all, he was a professor, and you know the esteem which titles carry in Germany, at least they still did in the sixties.

The unnerving rejection letters were climaxed, however, by a special event, the annual meeting of the Gruppe 47 in Princeton in 1968. It was, as usually, attended by the most famous German

critics and editors of lyrical works. Robert left for Princeton with
tremendous hopes. He was still sure he would find someone who
was of such discriminating taste that he would gladly accept the
poems for a book. On the first day of the meeting – shortly before it was Robert's turn, a young man, about 20 years of age
with a fancy sailor's cap (quite unusual for such a meeting) got
up and read from his "Publikumsbeschimpfung." It was Peter
Handke, and he stole the thunder, not just from Robert, but from
almost everyone else who was to read. I had been eagerly awaiting Robert's telephone call at home, but the phone did not ring.
Two days later he arrived home a dejected, depressed, totally different person than the one who had left for Princeton with such
high hopes. After Handke's tremendous, surprising success, everybody wanted to talk to him, nobody had been interested in
Robert.

Let me start with reading from a cycle of 16 poems on
Nürnberg, "Nürnberg wunderschöne Stadt." Some of them are
sarcastic, some admiring the city's beauty and history, some are
full of fear and hate.

No. 4 is titled "a nasty song."

he wore a little black coat
with a yellow star a pointed hat
his backpack filled
with colorful linens

at the gate he seemed lost
his hair covered his ears
they would not let him enter
their broad streets

"your name damned jew
you louse and swine?"
the guard shouted
he was such a man

"elieser ben des mordechai
with your permission great captain"
"from where have you come
you stinking scoundrel?"

"from Düsseldorf on the Rhine

i walked"
"what do you want in our beautiful town
you ass you cheap naked rat?"

"sell my goods"
"must pay me three silverlings
and when St. Lorenz chimes four
we'll close the gates behind you"

the sun was rising in the hillls
so he walked through the gate
it glowed over the roofs
and lit the rooms

the steeples were ablaze
against the sky like a fire
and boys and girls
chased after him

they sang high and low
so very German and so upright
"hey-hey jewboy
judas must die"

The following poem in the cycle "Nürnberg wunderschöne
Stadt" is

No. 5 "a noble song":

you are the crown of Frankonia
with jewels of diamonds rubies and gold
proudly you stretch in sunshine
you reveal splendor and might joy and fun

St. Lorenz St. Sebaldus churches are like pearls
they glitter beautifully in your hair
at the foot of your castle a stand of alder trees
graces the marvels of your beauty

the Cross rises from the center of this circle
on the castle's highest tower
beneath it stretches the city of festivals and dances

(5 more lines of description)

the princes often rode through your streets
the emperor encouraged the arts
the Swedes enjoyed your sausages
(1 more line)

have pity with the down-trodden the sick
a hospital build to help the poor
the jews however must be forced to leave
they all are guilty of the death of our Lord

No. 6 "burial song":

the city
which
was
our home
is dead

the mother
who
gave us birth
there
now covered
with loamy soil
in bohemia

raked
gassed
made into soap
silenced
no funeral procession
turns around
they say
the Plärrer (large square in Nürnberg)
burst
boiling hot
the Pegnitz (Nürnberg's river)
foamed
with blood
like the Nile
the castle
was ablaze

long
till it collapsed
the towers
mirrored fire-red
in the water

the angel
choked
howling
wild
and raw
from city-gate
to gate
decorated with swastikas
the shouts
shrill
high
through
small
alleyways
they
echo
in my ears

they are the voices
of my pale
family

they wear
a yellow star
they are
the servants
of the
dreadful
master

their eyes
are flashing
the teeth leering
through debris
and ruins

they walk revenge
revenge
their desperate
scream

yet
my mother
who screamed
in Auschwitz
was not among them

raked
gassed
made into soap
silenced
better to
forget it.

Robert had been looking forward to talking to the "Literatur-papst," Marcel Reich-Ranicki, but it was a brief and superficial conversation. Reich-Ranicki too, was only impressed by this new young Peter Handke. Robert's dream had not come true.

This was devastating to him. He was a proud man. And there was a lot of poetry published at that time, which was far less deserving of publication. The main fault of the non-acceptance of Robert's poetry was really the topic of its contents: Exile-Literature. Over the last 20 years, exile-literature has been gradually accepted. Exiled authors like Arno Reinfrank, Erich Fried, Hans Sahl, Rose Ausländer, to name just a few of the very many, published, but in the sixties, it was primarily Nelly Sachs, and the reason for this exception was probably that she had been awarded the Nobel Prize and was internationally known. When Robert wrote his poems it was not even a question of accepting or rejecting the contents of it, it was plainly a matter of not being heard.

The second deep disappointment with which he would have to grapple and was unable to solve was a political one. The United States was now involved in Vietnam. Robert had in the late sixties hired instructors and assistant professors because the Department had expanded rapidly, a fact of which he was very proud and rightly so. But being a kind and decent man, he did not anticipate that some of the new instructors and assistant professors were much more interested in politics than in teaching and research. It was inconceivable to him that young colleagues in his field were less or not at all eager to engage in professional research. Robert was not a stickler for duties, but he frowned upon the fact that some of these colleagues in his Department would rather march with students than prepare lectures. When he finally caught on and became aware of the fact that politics, not teaching, was the main concern of a number of the Department members who were really mean-spirited characters, he felt responsible for not having made good choices when hiring them, which, of course, was true.

In February of 1970, he received an invitation from the University of Florida in Gainesville to interview for a professorship there. We went together, but his greatest concern, which he expressed to me even before we arrived there, was "his" graduate students. He would repeatedly ask: "What will become of them, if I leave? Who will teach them instead of demonstrating and threatening to throw bombs on the campus?"

We returned to Houston, and when the offer from Gainesville arrived in the mail, he turned it down. "I cannot leave my students alone," was his explanation. I had advised him we should go, but it was mainly his pride that did not permit him to. It was as if the hate which he felt for the persecutors of his mother was now directed towards his own persecutors. And he was tired of fighting, tired of persecution. His love for his mother tore him apart. It seems he just wanted to be with her. He considered himself a failure as a poet; a failure as a chairperson. It got to the point where I was very concerned about his health, and I urged him to seek counseling, but he could not accept that either. He said to me: "Don't you see that I do not need a counselor, I do not want anything bad or harmful. It is this small group of instructors who is ill-intentioned and ill-prepared for their students. I do not need a psychiatrist, these malfeasants do." Of course, he was right. I cannot forget this sentence, because the word "malfeasants" was a new word for me.

If he had been recognized as a poet, or if he had been respected as a department chair as he was by colleagues at other universities (who invited him for lectures and for cooperation at the *Forster-Gesamtausgabe* in Berlin and the *Friedrich Schle-gel-Gesamtausgabe* with Ernst Behler and Hans Eichner, not to mention the various lectures he gave at the University of Texas in Austin), he might have recovered from this deep depression. He learned that academic and character short-comings of some of the teachers he had hired were turned into political issues. In order to hide their own shortcomings "wurden politische Süppchen gekocht."[34]

Cut-off from the world around them, Jews have often left the country where they were not welcome. But often a few were crushed by the pressure imposed upon them. Others fell into silence and isolation.[35] These were the days when he would speak more about his mother again. He was preoccupied with her suffering, her death. I tried to talk about faith. I read Job to him, but he remained an agnostic, torn between love, hate, and feelings of guilt. Abraham Joshua Heschel, who was expelled from Germany, returned to Warsaw, received a transit visa to London, and emigrated in 1940 to the United States, where he taught at Hebrew Union College in Cincinnati, said in his book "Man is not Alone" that moral activism, not cynicism or despair, should prevail.[36] But Robert, who did not believe, could not return to the religion of his childhood and youth. It might have been the crutch to help him to go on, if only he could be made to believe again.

He spoke a lot about his mother and saw her in his dreams. Had he kept his faith he would not have done what he did, but he was an agnostic and torn between loving and hating, "I hate this language, which I love." Finally, the longing to find peace, overwhelmed him. He was tired. His strength and his creativity were extinguished. There was no other choice for him but to join her.

Let me close with two more of his poems.

From the cycle "da wo wir stehen":

p. 63

there where we stand
one cannot stand any longer
there where we sit
one cannot sit any longer

there where we sleep
one cannot sleep any longer
there where we walk
one cannot walk any longer
there where we pray
one cannot pray any longer

Beginning "Schlußlied" (Last Song):

p. 59

The song
has ended
yet
i do
not
go home
the drums
are quiet
the sword
is
in the sheath
if only
it were
a plough
i can never
forget
i must always   (vergeben muß ich immer
forgive   vergessen kann ich nimmer)

Notes:

[1]Nadine Hauer, "Die verschwundenen Kinderjahre," *ZwischenWelten*, Wien, October 2001, p. 62.

[2]Primo Levi, *Collected Poems*, Faber and Faber, London, 1988, p. 9.

[3]Arnd Müller, *Geschichte der Juden in Nürnberg,* p. 184, 189, 197, 208.

[4]See Arnd Müller, p. 229.

[5]Letter by Susan Freudenthal, née Kahn, June 18, 1994.

[6]Adolf Diamant, *Chronik der Juden in Leipzig, Anfang, Vernichtung und Neuanfang*, Leipzig, 1933, p. 530.

[7]*Tonlose Lieder*, Darmstadt, 1978, p. 79

[8]These "Kindertransports were organized by the 'Cave of Children'-

Program and from December 1938 until September 1939, when the war broke out, about 10.000 children were shipped from Germany, Austria, Poland, and Czechoslovacia via Holland to England," in Jana Mikota, "Kinderleben im Exil," *ZwischenWelten*, Wien, 18. Jg., No. 3, Oct. 2001, p. 29.

[9]Job 7, 20.

[10]Hans Kailson, der in Berlin Medizin studierte und 1934 promovierte, war aber aufgrund der "Rassengesetze" nicht mehr in der Lage, seinen Beruf in Deutschland auszuführen. Er emigrierte 1936 nach Holland. Als Holland 1940 von deutschen Truppen besetzt wurde, mußte er untertauchen. Er sagte: "Die Rückkehr von extrem traumatisierten Kindern und Jugendlichen ist schwerer als jene von traumatisierten Erwachsenen. Seelisch schwer verwundete junge Menschen aufzufangen ist eine überfordernde Aufgabe .... Menschen, die in der Adoleszenz traumatisiert wurden, haben meist unter chronisch-reaktiven Depressionen zu leiden." *ZwischenWelten*, Wien, 18. Jg., No. 3, Oct. 2001, p. 73.

[11]Gedicht Rejzel Zychlinski in *Das Schweigewort hütet die Schicksalsspur. Ausgewählte Gedichte jüdischer Lyrikerinnen*, Jaizer, Berlin, 1994, p. 9.

[12]Igel Verlag, Paderborn, 1991.

[13]Igel Verlag, Paderborn, 1991, p. 62.

[14]Igel Verlag, Paderborn, 1991, p. 62.

[15]In *Das Schweigen hütet die Schicksalsspur*, Jaizer, Berlin, 1994.

[16]From *Tonlose Lieder*, Darmstadt, 1968, p. 77.

[17]See note 2, p. 8.

[18]Wolfgang Mieder, "Die Zeit hörte auf, alle Wunden zu heilen," in *Muttersprache*, no. 2, 1998, p. 149.

[19]Erwin Chargaff, *Abscheu vor der Weltgeschichte*, Klett-Cotta, 1988, p. 65.

[20]Roth still believed in a theist conviction when he says in a letter of March 22, 1933 to Stefan Zweig: "Man konnte das 6000jährige nicht jüdische verleugnen. Wir kommen eher aus der "Emanzipation", aus der Humanität, aus dem "Humanen" überhaupt, als aus Ägypten. Unsere Ahnen sind Goethe[,] Lessing[,] Herder nicht minder als Abraham, Isaac und Jacob." "Roths Politische Exilhaltung im Spiegel seiner Briefe," in Amy Colin/Elisabeth Strenger *Brücken über dem Abgrund*, München, 1994, p. 273.

[21]Robert L. Kahn: "Caroline and the Spirit of Weimar," *Modern Language Quarterly*, vol. 201, no. 3, 1959, pp.273-284.

[22]Robert L. Kahn, "Tieck's *Franz Sternbalds Wanderungen* and Novalis' *Heinrich von Ofterdingen*," *Studies in Romanticism*, Vol. VII, Autumn 1967, No. 1, pp. 40-63.

[23]Czeslaw Milosz, *Zeichen im Dunkel*, Suhrkamp, 1984, p. 102.

[24]*Tonlose Lieder*, Darmstadt, 1978, p.20.

[25]Kreuzer edited after Robert's death a "Teilnachdruck" of the Erstausgabe of Robert's *Tonlose Lieder* which contains also an epilogue by Käte Hamburger. It was published in 1986 by the Universität Gießen. In the epilogue of the booklet, Käte Hamburger calls Kahn's *Tonlose Lieder* a "großartigen Zyklus" and stresses their "Ton eines hintergründigen, bitteren, leidgeborenen Zynismus, der hier und da an den Heines gemahnt, doch nicht ohne Grund

bitterer als Heines, der von den unvorstellbaren Erfahrungen unseres Jahrhunderts noch nichts ahnen konnte." And she calls the volume's "Lieder" very appropriately "Zeigedichte der Moderne in einem sehr prägnanten Sinn."

[26]*Gebt unseren Worten nicht euren Sinn*, Rose Ausländer Stiftung, Köln 2001, p. 92.

[27]Quote by Muriel Ruckeyser in Alice Ostrik's essay, *Back to the Garden*, Profession 1992, p. 26

[28]*Poet's House*, New York, 1996, no p.

[29]*Sprache als Heimat*, Berlin, 1981, p. 12.

[30]See note 29.

[31]"Vom Zwielicht der Träume und Erinnerungen," in *Sprache als Heimat*, see note 29.

[32]*Tonlose Lieder*, Darmstadt, 1978, p. 25-27.

[33]See note 25.

[34]Hilde Domin, personal comment.

[35]Martin Gilbert, *Jews of Hope*, Viking 1983; it was meant as a response to Elie Wiesel's *The Jews of Silence*.

[36]See note 20, p. 251.

The Thread of Language through History:
From the Third Reich to the Present

Karin Doerr

Introduction

The fourteenth annual Harry H. Kahn Memorial Lecture was presented on March 31, 2003, and we were honored to welcome Prof. Karin Doerr from Concordia University at Montréal to the University of Vermont. She and her husband Prof. Gary Evans are frequent guests on our campus, and we appreciate their interest in our German and Holocaust programs.

It is a special delight to welcome our distinguished colleague and good friend Prof. Karin Doerr to the campus of the University of Vermont. Born and raised in post-war Germany, Prof. Doerr came to Canada in the 1970s. She has been teaching at Concordia University in Montréal for more than two decades, having received her B.A. degree in 1974 from Loyola University and both her M.A. and Ph.D. degrees from McGill University in 1978 and 1988 respectively. While she teaches primarily German language, culture, and literature, she has also very much been involved as a teacher in Women's Studies and the Holocaust. In fact, she is an Associate of the Montréal Institute for Genocide Studies, the Canadian Centre for Jewish Studies, and the Simone de Beauvoir Institute for Women's Studies.

Her numerous publications reflect these teaching interests. Of particular interest are her articles on "The Specter of Anti-Semitism in and around Annette von Droste-Hülshoff's *Judenbuche*" (1994), "Before the Holocaust: Teaching German Literature Containing Antisemitic Elements" (1999), "Memories of History: Women and the Holocaust in Autobiographical and Fictional Memoirs" (2000), "The Depiction of Auschwitz in an American Novel: Sherri Szeman's *The Kommandant's Mistress*" (2000), "The Nazi Period, the Holocaust, and German-Jewish Issues as Integral Subjects in a German Language Course" (2000), and "Germany's Language of Genocide at the Turn of the Century" (2002). One of her major contributions to the study of the language of the Holocaust was published right here at the University of Vermont. I speak of her revealing paper on "'To Each His Own' (*Jedem das Seine*): The (Mis-)Use of German Proverbs in Concentration Camps and Beyond" that appeared in *Proverbium: Yearbook of International Proverb Scholarship* (2000) with its gruesome pictures of the proverb "Arbeit macht frei" on concentration camp gates and other proverbs inscribed on supporting beams of the barracks.

But her *magnum opus* is clearly the invaluable book on *Nazi-Deutsch/Nazi German: An English Lexicon of the Language of the Third Reich* (Westport, Connecticut: Greenwood Press, 2002) that she co-authored with the historian Robert Michael. The two authors argue that the Nazi language, created and used as an instrument of coercion and indoctrination, reveals how the National Socialists ruled Germany and large parts of Europe, fought the Second World War, and committed crimes, mass murder, and genocide. Written from a socio-linguistic and historical point of view, the book presents an extensively researched dictionary of the language of the Third Reich. As such, it is an extremely important reference work for scholars, teachers, and students of the Nazi era, World War II, and the Holocaust. It represents the first and only comprehensive German-English dictionary of the language of the Third Reich, providing clear, concise, and informative definitions with important background information. The book contains many entries of specialized and charged vocabulary, including the terminology of Nazi ideology, propaganda slogans, military terms, ranks and offices, abbreviations and acronyms, euphemisms and code names, Germanized words, slang, chauvinistic and anti-Semitic vocabulary, as well as racist and sexist slurs. Robert Michael's major treatise on "The Tradition of Anti-Jewish Language" and Karin Doerr's superb discussion of "Nazi-Deutsch: An Ideological Language of Exclusion, Domination, and Annihilation" put the 6,500 dictionary entries into an historical and socio-linguistic framework. There is no doubt that this volume is an indispensable research tool, a handbook for any serious scholar or student of Nazi Germany, World War II, and the Holocaust.

Prof. Doerr's various research projects have been supported by Canadian government and university grants as well as by scholarships from the German Academic Exchange Program. Recently she has been extremely busy presenting lectures based on her significant research in Europe, Israel, Canada, and the United States. Much work has been done on the many aspects of the Holocaust, but the area of language and the Holocaust has not yet received the attention that it deserves. Such lecture titles as "The Impact of Language: Nazi German and Holocaust Survivors" (1998), "The Consequences of the Distortion of Language in the Third Reich" (1998), "The Persistence of Nazi German" (1999), "Remembering the Language of Genocide: Women and the Holocaust" (2000), "The Language of Discrimination and Persecution" (2000), "In Search of the Vocabulary of Genocide in German Dictionaries" (2000), "German Proverbs in the Third Reich and Beyond" (2000), "Retrieving Memories: Holocaust Survivors and the German Language" (2001), and "In the Voice of the Perpetrators: Presenting *Nazi Deutsch/Nazi German*" (2002) are clear indications of the thrust and importance of Prof. Doerr's work on the manipulative use of language by the Nazis and its effects on the many victims. Prof. Doerr has focused her scholarly investigations on the Nazi regime and how its members used, misused, and invented language in an attempt to invoke attitudes and claims of racial superiority among the German people and to ridicule, denigrate, and persecute Jews and other victims. As Prof. Doerr states in her book on Nazi German: "Nazi-Deutsch remains an indelible map of the intricate system under German National Socialism. This language has become an essential part of the academic discourse of Holocaust scholarship and it may even shed some light on the decades-old debate as to whether the Holocaust was an intentional Nazi objective or an evolving plan. As the twentieth century has passed into history, and its greatest catastrophe recedes further into the past, we need to assure that the generation of scholars and students, especially in English-speaking milieux, has access to the specialized language of the Third Reich that reflects its horrific ideological *Weltanschauung*. [...] Nazi-Deutsch reveals the incontrovertible fact of a criminal regime that was thriving in the heart of a once-civilized Europe" (pp. 41-42). The analysis of the

German language must be part and parcel of dealing with the Holocaust, and clearly the study of German as a foreign language is one major aspect of this requirement.

Lecture

The University of Vermont has been exemplary for creating a post-war bridge for the study of German and Jewish culture and history. This first drew me to one of your distinguished scholars, Wolfgang Mieder, German professor and expert in paremiology. What further links me to your institution is Raul Hilberg's Holocaust research, as well as my professional acquaintance with several of your previous guest speakers: Guy Stern, Sander Gilman, Ruth Klüger, and Lisa Kahn. They all foster a German-Jewish dialogue. Also, I have for years shared with friends and students the fine publications of The University of Vermont's Holocaust Center, including *The Holocaust Bulletin*. In 2001, my husband and I attended the Miller Symposium here. In short, UVM has been part of my academic orbit for some time. I, therefore, am especially honored by your invitation to deliver the 2003 Harry Kahn Memorial Lecture.

I did not have the privilege of knowing Harry Kahn whose academic and personal legacy attests to his love for both German literature and Jewish history. It is remarkable that he continued to adhere to the values of German humanistic education or *Bildung* in spite of forced exile from his homeland, Germany. I too originate from there and teach German in Canada as *Auslandsgermanistin* (professor of German abroad). As such, I am confronted with the dilemma of how to do justice to Johann Wolfgang von Goethe's famous moral imperative, "May man be honorable, helping, and good" (*"Edel sei der Mensch, hilfreich und gut!"*). In the wake of the Holocaust, this message can only be taught in conjunction with its violation. Through this prism, I see the oak tree near Weimar called "Goethe-Eiche" as a fitting symbol for German literature and culture after the Nazi era. The tree, located in the former Buchenwald concentration camp, was reduced to a mere stump during the war. Similarly, the National Socialists truncated and disfigured the German language.

Language in any society governs life in civil interaction, cultural expression, and general communication. It usually reflects a social reality that is based on ethical values. Language also carries discourses that are reactions to political and social developments. This may include expression of discontent or discrimination. For example, throughout the past centuries, anti-Jewish rhetoric was part of European culture. In nineteenth-century German politics, and mainly in response to Jewish Emancipation, a vociferous antisemitism became a familiar presence. Later, the Third Reich built on this presence and institutionalized an extreme agenda combining nationalism and antisemitism. By means of an effective use of propaganda, the Nazis appropriated, revised, and rearticulated language. In fact, they came to use language as an instrument that facilitated and concealed genocidal intentions and acts.

Karl Kraus and Victor Klemperer, as two individuals who were sensitive to shifts of language usage and meaning, noticed the Nazis' linguistic manipulations early on. Klemperer recorded the sometimes drastic and sometimes gradual transformation of German into a vernacular that he defined as *lingua tertii imperii*, coded as LTI, the language of the Third Reich.[1] From his vantage point as both language expert and German turned into targeted Jew, he demonstrated how this discourse permeated all levels of society and ranged from crass propaganda speeches to veiled statements, to seemingly innocuous exchanges with neighbors. It was indeed multifaceted, sometimes direct and offensive. It contained newly coined terms and old ones that were assigned new meanings. Today it is also called Nazi German and, seen in its entirety—particularly its often-secretive employment—it shows the fateful course the nation took. It has gained in importance retrospectively, reflecting Third Reich history in its linguistic framework.

In this lecture I shall focus on this vital role of language during the Nazi era and its effect on people's thinking, extending even beyond that criminal regime. I will also deal with its verbal representation (or absence) in present-day Germany and with language memories that distinguish the agents, spectators, and victims of the genocide. I shall demonstrate how language mirrors historically the revolutionary change in National Socialist

Germany and its social and military aggression spanning indoctrination and mass murder. Pointing first to the public slogans,
the most audible and prominent forms of expression by the Nazi
government, we note their effectiveness in disseminating ideo-
logically charged messages: "Men make history, we make men"
("*Männer machen Geschichte, wir machen die Manner!*") and
"You are nothing; your people is everything" ("*Du bist nichts,
dein Volk ist alles!*"). The first emphasized masculinity and glory
for boys selected to attend Hitler Youth training schools, while
the second, markedly different in tone and content, addressed
German schoolgirls predominantly. It urged them to submerge
personal identity into the pool of the greater community. Both
phrases reveal a sexist attitude together with a fundamental racism, the latter in the unstated but understood fact that they were
meant for "Aryan" Germans only.

Better known slogans, keywords, and concepts from that era
have left their traces in postwar German history and some of
them remain fixed iconographic Nazi symbols. By defining and
decoding them today, we expose their past significance and also
their hidden horror. As Nachman Blumenthal wrote shortly after
the Holocaust:

> Comprehension of the Nazi terminology is largely de-
> pendent upon understanding of the period in which it
> was created. Thus research into Nazi terminology must
> constitute an introduction to historical research. This is
> necessary in order to avoid wholesale deception and con-
> fusion of the terms coined and used by the Nazis ....[2]

He also warns against taking them at "their face value." Historical contextualization of this language reveals the sometimes hidden details of complex Third Reich events. To this purpose, our
English Lexicon of *Nazi Deutsch* (Nazi German) can be viewed
as an archeological tool that helps to unearth the connotative
meaning in order to transcend this "face value."[3] Further and
very importantly, it lays bare the verbal record of the genocidal
program that Berel Lang calls "the most explicitly articulated
and fully documented instance of the idea and the act of genocide."[4] The *Lexicon* provides first the literal meaning of the
terms, which hints at the mindset of their agents, and then translates them into contemporary English. The definition reveals the

camouflaged and misleading wording and the often-insidious intention behind it. For instance, the two terms *Volksgemeinschaft* and *Lebensraum*, at face value, seem to be easily understood as "community of people" and "living space." But they connote more than they state. In their specific Nazi context, they also represented the fundamental outlook and governing principles of the regime, which is that they were intended only for racially defined Germans. In addition, the words contained the unstated plan of future population transfers into and out of a Germanized territory, as well as the exclusion or elimination of others. As Omer Bartov says hyperbolically, the Germans' "'living space' became everyone else's 'killing space.'"[5]

Deconstructing the Third Reich language facilitates uncovering the developments that led to this historical reality. It lays bare the path towards Nazi Germany's achieving imperial objectives. For example, shortly after Hitler's accession to power, the regime embarked on an elaborate centralized coordination of the municipal governments. The term for this national control was taken from electro-technology, *Gleichschaltung*. It meant literally "simultaneous switching" onto the same current or wavelength, which was the Nazi view of the world and expressed in the already existing word *Weltanschauung*. This crucial political move made it possible to promote the agenda of "racial hygiene" (*Rassenhygiene*) in science, law, education, culture, and most other areas of influence. The basic idea was to "cleanse" (*reinigen*) the German blood and to end miscegenation in order to prevent a "racial stew" (*Rassenbrei*), as the Nazis called the mixing of German with non-German, particularly Jewish, blood. Such albeit fuzzy notions of race were applied in a new subject that was researched, taught, and promoted as *Rassenlehre* (racial doctrine).

This ideologically-infused race biology entered all educational spheres in Germany, from primary school books to youth activities, to preparations for motherhood, as well as to the soldier's life at the front. The examples of its verbalization range from *Der Giftpilz* ("The Toadstool" or "Poison Mushroom"), an antisemitic children's book published by *Der Stürmer* in 1938; to the *Heimabend* (club night), mandatory Wednesday-evening courses for *Hitlerjugend* (Hitler Youth) and *Bund deutscher*

Mädel (League of German Girls); the *Mütterschulung* (Mother schooling), the ideological and practical training to convince German women of the importance of mothering; and the *Richthefte des Oberkommanos der Wehrmacht*, the pro-German and antisemitic instructional booklets issued by the Defense Forces High Command. Although these National Socialist messages addressed different societal groups, they had two things in common: to promote a fraternal solidarity among Germans called "people's unity" (*Volkseinheit* or, more abstract and newly coined, *Volkheit*) and to alert them to or warn them of that which was "un-German" (*undeutsch*), either racially or spiritually.

Already in 1933, the student-organized book burnings were named "*Aktion wider den undeutschen Geist*" ("Action against the un-German spirit").[6] *Undeutsch* was also indirectly suggested with the well-known term "degenerate art" (*entartete Kunst*) that referred negatively to some art in Germany as modern, avantgarde, and, particularly, Jewish. One important adjective that described any undesirable influences on the German nation (*Volk*) in biological terms was "alien" (*artfremd*). It literally meant "alien to the [German] kind," which most of the time was understood to mean Jewish. The fight then against such "alien" intrusions on the German nation at any level was expressed as "struggle" (*Kampf*), "battle" (*Schlacht*), and "war" (*Krieg*), with "race war" (*Rassenkampf*) as a special, German mission. The so-called "drive to the east" (*Drang nach Osten*), with its forced territorial annexations, was therefore predicated upon a Darwinian struggle, to the death if necessary. This meant war in order to fight for the dystopian ideal of the Nazis' New European Order (*Neuordnung Europas*); hence, the military glorification of the "War of Liberation" (*Freiheitskrieg*). The concomitant use and eventual elimination of other people, i.e., eastern-European non-Germans viewed as "subhumans" (*Untermenschen*)—unlike the Jews who where seen as "race alien" (*rassefremd*), incompatible with the German race—was deemed a natural part of this effort. Parallel to raising the "Aryan" (*Arier*) to penultimate status was a revival and celebration of the mythical Germanic hero (*germanischer Held*) and cult of sacrificial death (*Opfertod*).

These pro-German developments resulted in numerous word formations, many of them centering on the prefixes *Deutsch-*, *nationalsozialistisch-*, *Reich-* and *Volk-*. All of them were intrinsically exclusionary. The National Socialists' preoccupation with race was particularly visible in the unusual, pseudo-scientific words linked to blood (*Blut*). There are alone fifty-one entries in our *Lexicon* that start with this word. They stand out in their unsettling emphasis as *Blutbewußtsein*, "blood consciousness," pride in, and awareness of, one's (German) blood; *blutgebunden,* "bound by blood," in the sense of belonging to a particular race; and negatively, *Blutvergiftung*, "poisoning of (German) blood," meaning the possible destruction of the German people by admixture and dilution with an alien race. The Hitler Youth motto, *Blut und Ehre* ("blood and honor"), engraved on their ceremonial knives, combined the notion of race and code of exemplary conduct that were believed unique to Germans. These two words can also be found in the infamous 1935 "Law for the Protection of German Blood and German Honor" (*Gesetz zum Schutze des deutschen Blutes und der deutschen Ehre*). One of its devastating effects for the Jews of Germany was the abrogation of citizenship. The abstract word *Ehre* stood for an all encompassing concept of "German" honor that was being inculcated in the young. Here is one example of the "sword words" (*Schwertworte*), the oath of Hitler Youth males, "Boys of the German Youth are hard, silent, and faithful. Boys of the German Youth are good comrades. The highest [achievement] for boys of the German Youth is honor" ("*Jungvolkjungen sind hart, schweigsam und treu. Jungvolkjungen sind Kameraden. Des Jungvolkjungen Höchstes ist die Ehre!*")[7] There were many different loyalty oaths (*Treueide*) that Germans, particularly the SS, had to swear. They all voiced devotion, personal responsibility, and sacrifice to the nation and to Hitler himself. This played a concrete role in the required *Bluteinsatz* (Blood operation), the German man's wartime duty to give even his life (When the war was already lost, military leaders on the eastern front ordered German soldiers to continue their last desperate resistance and thus caused hundreds and thousands more casualties). With a great deal of gallows humor, some of them referred to medals they received during these winter campaigns as *Gefrierfleischorden* ("Frozen-meat medal") or *Eisbeinorden* ("Frozen-bone [pig-knuckle] medal").

Other Nazi words, those pertaining to the elimination of "adversaries" (*Gegner*), have given rise to speculation and differing interpretations because their meanings shifted with the regime's evolving policies. These terms span the common, the despicable and direct, as well as the neutral or scientific. As early as 1933, *Ausschaltung* meant the exclusion of Jews from the civil service as decreed by the newly established "Aryan Clause" (*Arierparagraph*). This discriminatory law determined one Jewish grandparent to be sufficient to warrant the status of "non-German." This was their beginning of economic and professional strangulation, to which the German public was encouraged by the intimidating *Judenboykott* (Boycott of Jews). Over the years, Nazi officials expressed in many different ways their intention to eliminate or remove the Jews from German society and soil with words such as the disrespectful *abwandern* (to make go) and *Abschub* (shoving out); the direct, bureaucratic *Zwangsentjudungsverfahren* (forced removal of Jews); always the threatening and yet somewhat veiled *Abrechnung mit den Juden* (the settling of accounts with the Jews). Elimination as *Beseitigung*, literally "to do away with," stood also for incarceration or murder of political opponents, including Jews. Later, in the form of *Ausmerze* (extinction), it came to signify often the euthananized killings of institutionalized ill individuals—non-Jewish and Jewish Germans—under the name *T-4* or *Aktion T-4* (Operation T-4; this code referred to the Reich Chancellory address, *Tiergartenstraße* 4, in Berlin). The cold-blooded formulation of the 1920s German plan was "destruction of life unworthy of life" (*Vernichtung lebensunwerten Lebens*). Finally, elimination as *Ausscheidung*, *Ausmerze* (extinction), *Entfernung* (removal), among other terms, meant the expulsion or murder of people and peoples. For the Jews, such terms signified being singled out in a focused genocidal process.

The word *Weltjudentum* (World Jewry) had already negative connotations based on an alleged global conspiratorial power. More expressive and hateful were *Weltfeind* and *Weltpest*, the "enemy" or "plague of the world." Wolfgang Mieder has noted that the Nazis even invented antisemitic proverbs "dressed in the formulaic and rhymed pattern of proverb structures" to give their antisemitic message the aura of folk wisdom. He cites the following blunt and brutal example that has quasi-religious overtones: "Only when the last Jew has disappeared, / Will the folk find its salvation."[8] Needless to say, the German word *Jude* (Jew) by itself was derogatory and heavily burdened with centuries-old anti-Jewish stereotyping. It was even used as an insult for non-Jews, for instance in the adjectives *jüdisch* (Jewish) or *judenblind* (Jew-blind), which defined someone who was anti-government. The common address for Jews as *Jude X*, "Jew X (so-and-so)," the stamp *J(ude)* on all official documents, and finally the public marking with the yellow "Jew star" (*Judenstern*) became, once again, visible words and signs of otherness. In denying more than a century of cultural assimilation, the Nazis demonstrated verbally and visually the newfound (racial) dichotomy between "German" and "Jew." Objectification of Jews became law in Nazi Germany, and those Jews who had to wear the Star of David were referred to matter-of-factly by the name *Sternträger*, "bearer of a star." The fine sounding term could hardly disguise the fact that the Jews were now ostracized socially and abandoned legally within their own country.

Both language and history reveal the Nazi policy of targeting Jews as *Volksfeinde*, "enemies of country and people." There has been an ongoing debate as to whether the policy was evolutionary (functionalist) or deliberate (intentionalist).[9] One can argue that it evolved from social removal to one of intentional global annihilation. The varied and varying terms for "exclusion" or "elimination" may seem to tip the scale in favor of those advocating "functionalism." One can also argue that, from the onset of the regime in 1933, an "eliminationist antisemitism" existed, as evidenced by deliberately aiming at the destruction of the Jews at all levels of German government and society. Extreme propagandistic language, taken from the fight against disease, weeds and vermin, did indeed convey "eradication" and "extermination" of Jews with terms such as *Ausrottung* and *Vernichtung*. But it may have been understood by the public at the time as mere hyperbole, since such uncontrolled hate language had been part of the German antisemitic repertoire for decades if not centuries. Even if the primitive message in the 1940 antisemitic film, *Der Ewige Jude*, was "Get rid of the Jews," extinction of an entire people was generally considered outside of the thinking of a civilized nation.[10] With hindsight, we can now attribute genocidal intent to the Nazis once the official plan was decided in 1941. The fact that, after 1939, the Nazi government did not expel Jews any longer and, in 1941, issued a halt to emigration with the "emigration denial" (*Auswanderungsverbot*)—including from the German-occupied countries—in retrospect makes this development quite clear.

The Nazi regime saw the need to conceal the decision to commit genocide despite years of national and international indifference to Germany's legal and verbal violations as well as wholesale aggression against the Jews. Hence, *Endlösung* (Final Solution), today the recognizable keyword of the Holocaust, was not commonly known. Even when it was used, its surface meaning did not reveal the guarded secret plan. Instead, neutral and familiar terms, such as "resettlement" *(Umsiedlung)* and "evacuation" (*Aussiedlung* or *Evakuierung*) referred to the publicly visible removal of the Jews. Such terms conveyed the actual deportation of the Jews from their homeland—a spatial elimination that nobody could or would deny. But with the employment of these words, the Nazi regime masked the hidden new meaning, the intended destruction of the deportees. The systematic and ongoing train transports to German-occupied Poland were also called *Osttransporte* or, sometimes more specifically, *Judentransporte*.[11] Nevertheless, for most Germans they simply remained and have remained "transports." This way, there was no need to see beyond the neutral dictionary meaning and it was easier to accept the Jews' removal (*Entfernung*) from Germany.

Looking back at this Third Reich language, we see distinctly that verbal hook and crook aided the Nazi regime to succeed in its diabolic scheme. The camouflage provided perpetrators and onlookers with a linguistic shield. In addition, both the direct and disguised messages, aimed at the public, sometimes included a clever use of folklore and sayings. For example, one old adage, "To Each His Own" (*Jedem das Seine*), stood almost for the underlying principle that governed Hitler's Germany, since it accentuated the practiced difference between "us" and "them."[12] Often cited and prominently displayed on several concentration camp gates,[13] the Nazi meaning was two-fold, "beneficial for those in power and detrimental to those targeted."[14] For instance, the people ruthlessly incarcerated at Buchenwald, must have considered *Jedem das Seine* as a further mockery, since its script faced the inside of the concentration camp and was thus properly legible only from within. This and other gate inscriptions, usually in wrought iron—some of them displaying fine craftsmanship—have survived as lasting symbols of German perfidy. They have become icons of evil and are now part of the commemorative historic sites. The slogan at Auschwitz, *Arbeit macht frei*, is the most familiar trope and emblem of the Holocaust.[15] Its words represented a vicious irony produced by the Nazi mind, since we know of the deliberate "destruction through work" (*Vernichtung durch Arbeit*). Conversely, the reversal of the fundamental tenet of community, "Thou shalt not kill," was apparent in the name and insignia of the Death's Head (*Totenkopf*) of the *Waffen-SS* (Armed SS).[16] This symbol expressed the unfolding of the somber, terrible mystery of the relationship between death and the German destiny. The agents of death, in their role as the self-proclaimed German Lords (*Herrenmenschen*), acted like gods and violated the societal taboo of murder by using their power to obliterate life.

The veiled language of this premeditated human destruction is epitomized in the ultimate prototype of linguistic concealment, the secret protocol of the 1942 Wannsee Conference. A close reading of the text spells out the true objective of the top Nazi officials: It was to "comb (through)" (*durchkämmen*) Europe from West to East, collect Jews in "transit ghettos" (*Durchgangsghettos*), and work them "by natural reduction" (*natürliche Verminderung*) to death. The surviving Jews were called *Restbestand* (remaining stock), a term from economics. Since that remnant was deemed especially resilient, its subsequent annihilation was crucial. The protocol expresses this euphemistically with the term "treated accordingly" (*entsprechend behandelt*). The Nazis referred to this "final settlement" with another factual term from economics, the "Final Solution (to the Jewish Question)," or *Endlösung* (*der Judenfrage*).[17] Concealing the horrific idea of extinguishing an entire people, Omer Bartov observes that this term has "a bureaucratic ring, an administrative dimension, a military neatness; hence it also appears neutral."[18] All these characteristics lend a notion of distance and detachment. Berel Lang, after a long exercise of other linguistic possibilities, calls *Endlösung* "quite simply ... by an old name ...—that is, the lie."[19]

The practice of such camouflage was not arbitrary but rather part of a constantly changing set of language rules called *Sprachregelung*. During the war years, Nazi officials determined the words to be used or replaced. These were often common terms with undefined meanings that also allowed the users concealment. It was easier to say "special accommodation" (*Sonderunterbringung*), "special treatment" (*Sonderbehandlung*), or "special car" (*Sonderwagen*) instead of "mass murder," "execution," and "poison gas van." These were indeed Nazi lies, and the most wicked yet were the deceptions at the core of the Holocaust, in the killing facilities of the death camps. There, the signs in the anterooms of the poison gas chambers could read "shower room" (*Brausebad*) or "bath" (*Badeanstalt*). In addition, many false verbal assurances concealed from the helpless individuals the truth of imminent death. The purpose of these and the fake labels was to trick them into cooperation and to facilitate the perpetrators' killing task. The fact that the killers were often themselves unwilling Jewish victims told to kill or be killed, adds a horrifying twist to the Nazis' mechanized operation of human destruction. To turn these individuals into collaborators in crime reveals the despicable foundation of the thinking of the German agents who relegated them to the linguistically undefined category "Special Detachment" (*Sonderkommando*).

For this reason, Holocaust scholars need to reevaluate their liberal use of Nazi terminology, such as *Endlösung* or Final Solution when referring to the extinction of Jewish lives.[20] The danger of such language is that it may validate the perpetrators' mindset as well as their psychological and linguistic detachment from evil. Raul Hilberg was one of the first to refrain from employing either the crass or euphemistic distancing language of the perpetrators by calling the genocide *The Destruction of the European Jews*, as the title of his groundbreaking book illustrates.[21] Similarly, Berel Lang avoids the frequently used term "extermination" (*Vernichtung*) preferring instead the wording "the Nazi genocide against the Jews" and clearly names the murderers as well as their victims with this concrete phrasing.

As we may surmise, the Jews came to figure prominently in the *Lexicon* that Robert Michael and I began with the intention to document the range and scope of the Third Reich language. We ended up creating lexical order out of terms that not only manifested racism and military aggression but also gross violations of human rights, particularly the genocide. It became evident that the Nazis' preoccupation with the Jews, their persecution, and eventual annihilation, is mirrored in their language throughout. Inadvertently, our *Lexicon* crystallizes this fact, since there is hardly a page that misses a reference to them. Gitta Sereny, too, had to admit about her recent book, *The German Trauma*, "I have been struck and—I say it frankly—somewhat disturbed by how much of it came to revolve around the murder of the Jews."[22] In the *Lexicon*, even the first and last entries happen to concern themselves with the judeocide: "*A*" is the abbreviation of *Arbeitsjuden*, or "work Jews," and *Zyklon-B* the deadly cyanide gas. *Arbeitsjuden* stood for Jews capable of work for the German war industry, ultimately to be worked to death, and *Zyklon-B* for the gas that was used to kill countless Jewish men, women, and children in specially designed gas chambers. The intended victims were also referred to by the Nazi euphemism, "the material for the Jewish resettlement" (*Material für die Judenumsiedlung*), as well as other dehumanizing terms like "pieces" (*Stücke*) and "figures" (*Figuren*) instead of "Menschen," "individuals," or simply, "Jews." The two entries, "*A* " and *Zyklon-B*—in their unintended chronology—make fitting linguistic bookends to this compilation of Nazi terms and underscore the truism that World War II was as much a war against the Jews as it was a war of German conquest. History further underlines this fact when focusing on the *Wehrmacht* (German Army) moving east and the *Einsatzgruppen* following suit. It is well documented that the task of the latter, from beginning to end, was to round up and murder Jewish civilians.[23] They were therefore Mobile SS killing units called vaguely *Einsatzgruppen*, "Special Task Groups," that hunted down "partisans" or "resisters." But in the top-secret reports that read like business balance sheets, we also find the truth: The overwhelming numbers of victims were recorded there as having been Jews.[24]

Decades after the Nazi period, we are left and obliged to ask what happened to this Niagara of Nazi German terms. Since many Germans viewed the end of the regime, May 7, 1945, as

Stunde Null (zero hour) or *Nullpunkt* (point zero), it signified to
them a new beginning. The ensuing political "denazification"
meant also "cleansing" the language of its Nazi jargon, style, and
most obvious references.[25] The Basic Law of the new Federal
Republic codified outlawing open expression of National Socialist ideas as well as antisemitism. But the Germans' rebuilding of
their country that lay in ruins, can be viewed as burying the past
as well.[26] When the terminology of the genocide in its specific
Nazi wording surfaced during the Nuremberg war-crime trials, it
needed to be decoded and translated. Although many of the
terms stayed in the German language, they have remained veri-
table social taboos. It is perhaps for this reason that they cannot
readily be traced in contemporary standard German (or bilingual)
dictionaries. In a focused study of postwar dictionaries, Kurt
Jonassohn and I checked four familiar words that comprise the
Nazis' systematic procedure of the annihilation of the Jews: *Aktion, Umsiedlung, Selektion,* and *Endlösung.*[27] We noticed a distinct inconsistency in the inclusion of these words with their full
Nazi connotations. With exceptions of specialized glossaries, the
overall tendency is to leave them ambivalent and ill defined.[28]
Yet, their distinct genocidal meanings are a part of Germany's
national memory and an usually unspoken legacy of the past.

We are better able to ascertain what happened to the German
proverbs that the Nazis had misused or reduced to a deadly liter-
alness, such as *Leben und leben lassen* (Live and let live). Germans have reassigned them their traditional meanings and today
use them freely. This includes *Jedem das Seine* (To each his
own) in contemporary German advertisements by McDonald's,
Burger King, Nokia, and others. Nokia had the temerity to post
its ad with this phrase on the fence surrounding the construction
site for the Berlin Holocaust memorial. After protests, the company apologized for the "unfortunate choice of words" and replaced them promptly with Shakespeare's "As you like it" *(Was
ihr wollt)*. A spokesperson for the American Jewish Committee
(AJC) called the situation "void of history" *(geschichtslos)* and a
"mockery" *(Verhöhnung)* of Holocaust victims.[29] This was a protest against the erasure of history and memory. The controversy
around the public display of "To each his own" illustrates that
the phrase is tainted by its Nazi use. Yet, German dictionaries
and phrase books sometimes list this and other sayings without

reference to their historic disgrace or omit them altogether. With such inconsistencies in the historical record so far, we can only hope for a rectification in the future, so that we will obtain a complete view of the impact of Germany's Nazi history, as much on its language as on the expression of folk wisdom.[30]

Another question remains with regard to language memories of those who bore the brunt of the Nazi terror. For instance, at what point did concentration camp inmates realize the falsehood behind the German words on the gate inscriptions? Pertaining to *Arbeit macht frei*, some survivors maintain that no one was fooled by it. Other testimonies reveal that the words' promise of freedom helped them to survive. But for many German-Jewish survivors, moral imperatives, such as *Sei ehrlich!* ("Be honest") or sayings like *Ehrlich währt am längsten* ("Honesty is of long duration"), have remained a most cruel barb. Ruth Klüger writes: "German proverbs have been an abomination for me ever since, I can't listen to a single one of them without imagining it on the crossbeam of a concentration camp barracks ...."[31] She recalls with cynicism other old German sayings and maxims, "Speech is silver, silence is gold" (*Reden ist Silber, Schweigen ist Gold*) and "Live and let live" (*Leben und leben lassen*) that were carved onto the rafter beams at Auschwitz-Birkenau. The young Klüger could not comprehend their function in the *Lager* (camp) because they were simply out of place: "I stared at them every day, disgusted by their absolute claim of truth, which this reality revealed to be a total lie."[32]

Other German-Jewish survivors experienced how their German mother tongue had turned into a language of exclusion and persecution. They remember its linguistic manifestations from virtually all media and official discourse. Klemperer recalled bitterly being addressed as "*der Jude Klemperer*" ("the Jew Klemperer," *LTI*, 103). For him and many other German-Jews who survived in hiding, 19 September 1941 was the "worst day ... in the twelve years of hell," as they were forced to wear the official marking to which he referred as "the yellow rag with the black imprint: '*Jew*'" ("*der gelbe Lappen mit dem schwarzen Aufdruck: 'Jude'*").[33]

Many Jews under German hegemony outside of Germany suffered the speech of the German perpetrators. This included public notices and official documents as well as personal interactions. In numerous cases, when one is reading non-German survivors' accounts, the reader's eye is immediately drawn to those German words in italics that are immortalized in their unambiguous viciousness. These are often the basest insults and expletives by SS officials or German and Austrian soldiers. To this day, Holocaust survivors cite them with a chilling familiarity and make a distinction between the enemies' German and their own language. For many, the sound of German, even today, is equated with baseness, atrocities and murder, and can hurl them emotionally back into the war.[34]

One can only wonder how Germans remember these words as perpetrators or bystanders. Since they have remained in their cultural and linguistic environment, Germans have not only contributed to language change and renewal, but have also silenced and even revised some Third Reich terms. Here it becomes evident that contrasting recollections of the victors and the vanquished manifest "parallel histories," as well as confluent memories.[35] In Germany, there has also been a noticeable absence of focusing on the Jews as the Nazi victims in favor of the Germans' own status as *Kriegsopfer*, "war victims."[36] Thus, they also have blocked out memories of hate speech and the threatening discriminatory vocabulary that was ubiquitous during the Nazi era. Perhaps one of the reasons is that "the primal impulses" and the "hatreds and enmities ... are transmitted" through language after they have become part of the speakers' consciousness.[37] We recall the undeniable public signs of "No Jews and dogs allowed" (*Für Juden und Hunde verboten*); buildings labeled "Jew-houses" (*Judenhäuser*); and doorbell signs with the obligatory reference *Jude* in front of a name. There was also the color "Jew yellow" (*Judengelb*); the evident "Jew star" (*Judenstern*), the Star of David; the yellow park benches designated "for Jews only" (*nur für Juden*); and, finally, the yellow triangles for those Jews who were not killed immediately upon arrival at a concentration camp. Despite such obvious and visual language references of the past, it is not easy to obtain statements from Germans that refer to them. They avoid also the word *Jude* (Jew) due to its connotative burden. Germans tend to refrain as well from expressing openly memories of Nazi sentiments like *Herrenvolk* (master race) and past loyalty to their often-beloved

Führer (Hitler as their leader). But it would be a mistake to imagine that they forgot all this and the manifestations of exclusion of their (Jewish) citizens and neighbors who had "disappeared" (*waren weg*), that is, were removed (*entfernt*) from the social environment.

Most of the words from the Third Reich language highlighted in this lecture were part of the reality and therefore part of the contemporary discourse of Nazi Germany and its people. This underscores the fact that National Socialist thought and many of its actions were openly verbalized. Yet it is clear that such a concrete physical and psychological presence in German life under Nazism was deliberately suppressed after the collapse of the regime. Perhaps for this reason, some Germans still cling to the neutral and "face-value" meaning of some Nazi terminology and thus continue to ignore its full connotations. Bartov calls this "national amnesia camouflaged by euphemisms of distance and strangeness."[38] It seems, linguistic Third Reich history remains in a quiet corner of the collective German memory. Primo Levi's judgment is harsher when he contends that the "rememberer has decided not to remember, and has succeeded: by dint of denying its existence, he has expelled the harmful memory as one expels an excretion or a parasite."[39] Levi's words likely carry a deliberate echo of the Nazis' reductive language that objectified Jews. With the phenomenon of German "forgetting" we must not underestimate the factor of shame present in the perpetrator nation. Berel Lang reminds us of the initial silence shortly after war's end:

> Some of that first silence was willed: the survivors stopping for breath and looking, incredulously, at the promise of a future; the spectators, taken by shame at the end of a tragedy in which they suddenly discovered themselves as actors; the agents of genocide hoping to forget or, more often, to be forgotten. But much of it was a reflex, an exclamation without sound: history, for once, was at a loss for words.[40]

But the German case makes clear that if history is repressed there cannot be an expression of its memory. Ironically, it had been the intention of the Third Reich leaders to erase all traces of the genocide, precisely so that there would be no historical record or memory of it. But in fact, verbal remnants from the Nazi period persist as tenacious reminders of that history. The language of genocide could and did not disappear with the last murders. Instead, word prints of the past have left imprints on the present because of the monstrousness of the deed that will not go away.

If many of these terms are no longer acceptable in general German usage today, one consequence based on history and the German war trauma, has been the generation of a new German terminology. With few exceptions, it also appears vague, like its Nazi German counterpart, yet is commonly understood. Take the simple term "past" (*Vergangenheit*), which is often employed in Germany as meaning "the Nazi period" (*die Nazizeit*). It reappears in the over-quoted compound *Vergangenheitsbewältigung*, which is "coming to terms with the Nazi years." Erna Paris calls it a "lofty ideal that is doomed to failure, and not just because of the immensity of Nazi crimes. For the past, it seems, can never be overcome. It lurks forever in memory. … loiters in cemeteries."[41] A bold term, *Aktion Sühnezeichen* or "Operation Sign of Atonement," was coined in 1959. It was the name of an association formed at the initiative of mainly young Protestant Christians in East and West Germany that wanted to demonstrate recognition of German war crimes committed particularly against Poland. It resonates the Nazis' infamous "Actions" (*Aktionen*), the vicious assaults against the Jews that accompanied wartime conquests. It could be argued that *Aktion Sühnezeichen* was meant to overwrite this connotation. Ironically, its founders did not emphasize the genocide against the Jews.

Another term, *Wiedergutmachung*, arose from Germany's admission of past wrong—something that cannot be said about all perpetrator nations. Its literal meaning is "to make good again." Although we know that it is impossible to right a catastrophe such as the Holocaust with money or new laws, there is at least the country's official attempt and recognition of the crimes against humanity as it tries to build bridges between Germans and Jews and former enemy countries. Of course there are those who prefer to draw a "final line" under this chapter of German history. This is expressed in the word *Schlußstrich*, and the discussion around this topic is the often-heated *Schlußstrichdebatte*.

Many of these linguistic formations and their usage illustrate an ambivalent connectedness between words, history, and memory. Controversial verbalizations or circumventive representation often speak volumes. In this sense, American *Germanist* Ernestine Schlant assessed Germany's mainstream postwar literature vis-à-vis the Holocaust as "a literature of absence and silence contoured by language." She sees such evasive cultural expression as a "seismograph of a people's moral positions."[42] Bartov concurs with this assessment: "What is notable about these works [by Böll, Grass, and Lenz] is not merely the fact that all Germans end up in them as victims, but that there are no other victims but Germans. This is what I would call an absence of representation."[43]

It is this kind of omission or apparent "forgetfulness" that mars many other German efforts focussing on the Nazi past. At the same time, we must acknowledge the changes in Germany. In 1995, the Fritz Bauer Institute in Frankfurt am Main opened and is devoted to Jewish History and Holocaust Studies. Also, the first chair in Holocaust Studies was established at the university of Giessen in Hesse. We need to include the word "Holocaust" as one of the new terms in the German language that has only recently been officially accepted as valid for the judeocide. There is increased scholarly preoccupation with the subject in the form of historical and local community studies. One such example is the recent installation art project by Renata Stih and Frieder Schnock. Its title is *Places of Remembrance* (*Orte des Erinnerns*) and it deals with words and images.[44] In an area of Berlin that once had a large Jewish population, the artists displayed verbal messages from every-day life during the Nazi era. They posted texts of rules and regulations passed between 1933 and 1945, pointing publicly to the historic reality of Germany's persecution of Jews and thus forcing the viewers to remember its verbalization. The artists used examples of the Nazis' language to admonish and to warn of the unconcealed erosion of basic human rights that could occur again simply because it happened before.

A different art project is the famous 1986 column in Harburg-Hamburg by Jochen Gerz (*Mahnmal gegen Faschismus*), designed to slowly disappear into the ground after visitors have inscribed it with their own words about the past.[45] This monument, nonetheless, could be seen as another manifestation of momentarily signal a presence but ultimately to bury it. Its viewers thus determine whether memory traces are left or not. The question then remains as to whether such art succeeds or fails in commemorating the Shoah and whether it teaches us anything about German history except it may be best to make it disappear. In the end there is nothing left, not even words. They, too, are underground and thus this inscribed column becomes a symbol of Germany's buried collective Holocaust memory.

In conclusion, I wish to return once more to the Third Reich and two internationally familiar Nazi adjectives. They were used to proclaim the success in one of the Nazis' most important objectives, to make Germany and indeed the world, *judenrein* or *judenfrei*, "cleansed" or "free of Jews." Signs with these words were openly displayed on buildings and village entrances to advertise the achievement of this official racial "cleansing," which would today be called "ethnic cleansing." But even the words "clean" and "free" are, in their basic denotative meaning, suggestive of a desirable state. They did not literally account for the dirty acts of mass deportations and wholesale murder of Jewish communities. Yet, as much as the Nazis hoped to reach their utopian biological goal of *judenrein*, the many references to Jews in the *Lexicon of the Third Reich Language* reveal their continuing presence in the Nazis' frenzied preoccupation with them and, finally, their genocidal intention. Perhaps as silent witnesses, these entries can assume the role of linguistic tombstones for the countless anonymous victims. If we flip the German idiom, "a fabricated story from A-Z" ("*von A-Z erfunden*"), the *Lexicon* uncovers, literally from A-Z, no fabrication, but a historical reality as well as facts hidden behind many words that were meant to conceal and deceive. Therefore, our work illuminates the underlying *leitmotif* expressed in Victor Klemperer's adapted idiom and underscored by Wolfgang Mieder, *in lingua veritas* ("in language lies the truth").[46]

The Nazi German *Lexicon* demonstrates the importance of the role of language in history, especially its use in the genocide. Words still need to be decoded, reworked, and defined in order to show their hidden and ideologically-colored meaning. The thread of the Third Reich language is still visible in our time. Its presence signifies its influence in the past, which has remained relevant for us today, beyond officially organized commemoration. In this way, Nazi German demands to be noticed and reckoned with in both scholarly and human discourse. We need to draw attention to the connectedness of language, ideology, and political actions and apply the insights gained from such knowledge.[47]

Notes:

[1]Viktor Klemperer, *L(Lingua) T(Tertii) I(Imperii): Notizbuch eines Philologen* (Leipzig: Reclam, 1996). All further references under *LTI.*

[2]"On the Nazi Vocabulary," in *Yad Vashem Studies: on the European Jewish Catastrophe and Resistance,* 1 (Jerusalem: Jerusalem Post Press, 1957), 65.

[3]Robert Michael and Karin Doerr, *Nazi-Deutsch/Nazi German: An English Lexicon of the Language of the Third Reich* (Newport, CT: Greenwood Press, 2002). All further references under *Lexicon.*

[4]Berel Lang, *Act and Idea in the Nazi Genocide* (1999; rpt. Syracuse NY: University Press, 2003), 14. Further references under Lang.

[5]Omer Bartov, *Germany's War and the Holocaust: Disputed Histories* (Ithaca, NY: Cornell University Press, 2003) 85. Further references to this edition under Bartov, *Germany's War.*

[6]The student leader in Bonn, Walter Schlevogt, demanded "the eradication of all un-German intellectual products" (*"Ausrottung aller undeutschen Geistesproduktion"*). See Karl-Heinz Joachim Schoeps, *Literatur im Dritten Reich 1933-1945* (Berlin: Weidler, 2000), 44, 66.

[7]*Lexicon,* 369.

[8](*"Erst wenn der letzte Jude ist verschwunden, / Hat das Volk seine Erlösung gefunden"*) in *Proverbs are Never Out of Season: Popular Wisdom in the Modern Age* (Oxford: UP, 1993), 249. See also "'...As if I Were the Master of the Situation': Proverbial Manipulation in Adolf Hitler's *Mein Kampf*," in *The Politics of Proverbs* (Madison, WI: U of Wisconsin P, 1997), 9-38.

[9]Two important representative works on these views, respectively, are Aly, Götz. *"Final Solution": Nazi Population Policy and the Murder of the European Jews.* Trans. Belinda Cooper and Allison Brown. London: Arnold, 1999. [From the German *"Endlösung": Völkerverschiebung und der Mord an den europäischen Juden.* Frankfurt/M: S. Fischer, 1995.], and Daniel Jonah Goldhagen, *Hitler's Willing Executioners: Ordinary Germans and The Holocaust* (New York: Knopf, 1996).

[10]Stig Hornshøj-Møller, *"Der ewige Jude": Quellenkritische Analyse eines antisemitischen Propagandafilms* (Göttingen: Institut für den Wissenschaftlichen Film, 1995).

[11]For extensive information on the transports, its trains, and terminology, see Raul Hilberg, *Sources of Holocaust Research* (Chicago: Ivan R. Dee,

2001), and Raul Hilberg, *Sonderzüge nach Auschwitz* (Frankfurt/M: Ullstein, 1987).

[12]For a discussion of "us" versus "them" in this context, see Frederic D. Homer, *Primo Levi and the Politics of Survival* (Columbia: University of Missouri Press, 2001), 61.

[13]This practice was most likely initiated by Dachau camp Kommandant and chief inspector of all concentration camps, Theodor Eicke. He "had his letter-head printed with the chilling words: 'The only thing that counts is an order'" (*"Es gibt nur eines, das Gültigkeit hat: der Befehl!"*). Quoted from Dirk Reinartz and Christian von Krockow, trans. from the German Ishbel Flett, *Totenstill* (New York: Scalo, 1995), 19.

[14]See Karin Doerr, "'To Each His Own' (*Jedem das Seine*): The (Mis-)use of German Proverbs in Concentration Camps and Beyond," in *Proverbium: Yearbook of International Proverb Scholarship*. Vol. 17 (University of Vermont: 2000), 71-90. Further citations from this article under Doerr, "To Each His Own."

[15]See *Dictionary of the Holocaust: Biography, Geography, and Terminology*, Eric Joseph Epstein and Philip Rosen, eds. (Westport, CT: Greenwood P, 1997), 76; see also Deborah Dwork and Robert Jan van Pelt, *Auschwitz: 1270 to the Present* (New York: W.W. Norton, 1996), 102.

[16]After 1936, their official designation was the *SS-Totenkopfverband* (SS Death Head Unit), *Lexicon*, 384.

[17]The text of the protocol is reproduced in *The Holocaust: Selected Documents in Eighteen Volumes*, John Mendelsohn, ed.,vol. 11: *The Wannsee Protocol and a 1944 Report on Auschwitz by the Office of Strategic Services* (New York: Garland, 1982), 3-17.

[18]Omer Bartov, "Antisemitism, the Holocaust, and Reinterpretation of National Socialism," in *The Holocaust and History: The Known, the Unknown, the Disputed, and the Reexamined*, Michael Berenbaum and Abraham J. Peck, eds. (Bloomington, IN: Indiana University Press, 2002), 80.

[19]See "Language and Genocide," in *Act and Idea in the Nazi Genocide* (Chicago: University of Chicago Press, 1990), 91.

[20]See Randolph L. Braham, ed. *The Treatment of the Holocaust in Textbooks: The Federal Republic of Germany, Israel, The United States of America* (New York: Columbia University Press, 1987). As Bartov mentions, "German scholars tend to put such terms as 'Final Solution' or 'Fuehrer' in inverted commas, lest readers take them literally, and also to indicate their own distance from the Nazi vocabulary." Bartov, *Germany's War*, 85.

[21]Raul Hilberg, *The Destruction of the European Jews*, Vol. 3 (New York: Holmes & Meier, 1985).

[22]*The German Trauma: Experiences and Reflections 1938-2000* (Allen Lane: Penguin P. 2000), xiv.

[23]Christopher R. Browning, *Ordinary Men: Reserve Police Battalion 101 and the Final Solution in Poland* (New York: Harper Collins, 1992).

[24]Top Secret Document PS-2076/41 (No. 1 and 2) Kaunas, 10 December 1941; "Jäger Report," *Jäger-Bericht*, 10 Dec. 1941, written by SS Colonel Karl Jäger, the commander of SS/SD Einsatzkommando 3 in charge of the killings

in Lithuania. He presented the day-by-day listings of those shot by his detachment and Lithuanian police units between 4 July and 17 October 1941. For example, "Einsatzkommando 3, 254 Jews, 42 Jewesses, 1 Polish comm., 2 Lithuanian NKVD agents, 1 mayor of Jonava who gave the order to burn the city of Jonava."

[25]As one of the numerous publications on the subject, see Constantine FitzGibbon, *Denazification* (London: Michael Joseph, 1969).

[26]This topic is discussed in *Revisiting Zero Hour 1945: The Emergence of Postwar German Culture*, Stephen Brockmann and Frank Trommler, eds. (Washington DC: Johns Hopkins University, 1996).

[27]Karin Doerr and Kurt Jonassohn, "Germany's Language of Genocide at the Turn of the Century," in *The Century of Genocide: Selected Papers from the 30th Anniversary Conference of the Annual Scholars' Conference on the Holocaust and the Churches*, Daniel J. Curran, JR., Richard Libowitz, and Marcia Sachs Littell eds. (Merion Station, PA: Merion Westfield P International, 2002), 27-48; see also Gertrud Mackprang Baer, *In the Shadow of Silence* (Toronto, ON: Harper Collins, 2002), 309-310; and Gabrielle Hogan-Brun, *National Varieties of German outside Germany: A European Perspective* (Oxford: Peter Lang, 2000).

[28]New German dictionary editions are in the process of being written. They may address and rectify these shortcomings. Unfortunately, the 1999 Duden edition does not seem to have solved the problem.

[29]Similarly, representatives of Burger King had to retract their leaflets with *Jedem das Seine* in the town of Erfurt, and the "head of the Buchenwald Memorial Center said that the ad was inexcusably stupid." See report in *Jerusalem Post* (7 June, 1999).

[30]Doerr, "To Each His Own," 85.

[31]("*Mir sind deutsche Sprichwörter seither ein Greuel, ich kann keines kören, ohne es mir auf dem Querbalken einer KZ-Baracke vorzustellen und es sofort mit einer abwertenden Bemerkung zu entkräften.*") *weiter leben. Eine Jugend* (Göttingen: Wallstein, 1992), 119. All translations from the German are my own. Further references to this text under Klüger.

[32]("*Ich starrte sie täglich an, angewidert von ihrem absoluten Wahrheitsanspruch, den diese Wirklichkeit als totale Lüge bloßstellte.*") Klüger, 119.

[33]("*Welches war der schwerste Tag der Juden in den zwölf Höllenjahren? Nie habe ich von mir, nie von anderen eine andere Antwort erhalten als diese: der 19. September 1941. Von da an war der Judenstern zu tragen, der sechszackige Davidstern, der Lappen in der gelben Farbe, die heute noch Pest und Quarantäne bedeutet und die im Mittelalter die Kennfarbe der Juden war, die Farbe des Neides und der ins Blut getretenen Galle, die Farbe des zu meidenden Bösen; der gelbe Lappen mit dem schwarzen Aufdruck: 'Jude'....*") LTI, 213.

[34]See Karin Doerr, "Etched in Memory: Survivors and the Language of Genocide," in *Holocaust Bulletin* (Burlington, VT: University of Vermont, Spring 2003), 5-6.

[35]Saul Friedländer, *Memory, History, and the Extermination of the Jews of*

Europe (Bloomington and Indianapolis: Indiana UP, 1993), 93.

[36]"... the representation of absence is arguably one of the most crucial tropes in German literary, cinematic, and scholarly representations of recent German history," Bartov, *Germany's War*, 217.

[37]Herbert Hirsch, *Genocide and the Politics of Memory: Studying Death to Preserve Life* (Chapel Hill : University of North Carolina P, 1995), 97-98.

[38]Bartov, *Germany's War*, 170.

[39]Primo Levi, *If This is a Man and The Truce*, trans. Stuart Woolf (London: Abacus, 1987), 17.

[40]Lang, 229.

[41]"The Germans call it *Vergangenheitsbewältigung*: mastering, or overcoming, the past.... It shelters behind beautifully painted movable screens. The past can only be managed. With remembrance. With accountability. With justice–however frail, however inadequate, however imperfect." Erna Paris, *Long Shadows: Truth, Lies, and History* (New York: Bloomsbury, 2001), 464.

[42]Ernestine Schlant, *The Language of Silence: West German Literature and the Holocaust* (New York: Routledge, 1999), 1. Even two acclaimed recent German novels, Bernhard Schlink, *The Reader*, trans. Carol Brown Janeway (1995; New York: Random House, 1998), and Günter Grass, *Crabwalk* (Göttingen: Steidl, 2002) are marred by German hegemony over history as well as its memory and the depiction of Germans as victims rather than focussing with the same compassion on the Jewish victims.

[43]Bartov, *Germany's War*, 226.

[44]Renata Stih and Frieder Schnock, *Orte des Erinnerns, Places of Remembrance*, Catalogue (Berlin: Haude and Spenersche Verlagsbuchhandlung, 2002).

[45]Jochen Gerz, "Memory and Mimesis," Symposium Memory and Archive (Montreal: 23-25 March, 2000).

[46]See Wolfgang Mieder, "*In lingua veritas:"Sprichwörtliche Rhetorik in Victor Klemperer's "Tagebüchern 1933-1945"* (Wien: Edition Praesens, 2000).

[47]I wish to thank Gary Evans for his valuable help with the manuscript.

Recuperating Unheard Voices:
German Jewish Poetry after Auschwitz

Jack Zipes

Introduction

The fifteenth annual Harry H. Kahn Memorial Lecture took place on April 8, 2004, and we were pleased to welcome Prof. Jack Zipes from the University of Minnesota to our campus. It had been our wish for a number of years to have this engaged scholar and friend come to our campus, and it was appreciated that he presented a second lecture on fairy tales.

It is a most welcome task to welcome our renowned colleague and good friend Prof. Jack Zipes to the campus of the University of Vermont. Prof. Zipes graduated from Dartmouth College in 1959 and received his M.A. degree one year later from Columbia University. In 1965 he obtained his Ph.D. degree from that institution and began his influential career as a German professor that has taken him to New York University, the University of Wisconsin at Milwaukee, the University of Florida, and the University of Minnesota, where he has recently completed a three-year term as the Director of the Center for German and European Studies.

His courses and research are primarily concerned with critical theory, the Brothers Grimm, fairy tales, folklore, children's literature, theater, and contemporary German literature with an emphasis on the Holocaust and German-Jewish cultural relations. He is himself an award-winning storyteller in public schools and has done exciting work with various children's theaters. It is this community outreach to youngsters that has made his superb scholarship accessible to hundreds of youngsters, who have benefitted greatly from his scholarly expertise and artistic gift of letting narratives come alive through oral performance.

Scholars of the European fairy tale tradition will doubtlessly agree that Prof. Zipes is the leading scholar in this fascinating field in North America, having made available numerous invaluable studies and translations in his almost forty-year long career as a leading scholar of German and comparative literature. There is no way that I can mention all of his books, but let me at least cite a few titles to illustrate his wide range of interest: *Breaking the Magic Spell: Radical Theories of Folk and Fairy Tales* (1979), *Fairy Tales and the Art of Subversion: The Classical Genre for Children and the Process of Civilization* (1983), *Trials and Tribulations of Little Red Riding Hood: Versions of the Tale in Sociocultural Context* (1983), *The Brothers Grimm: From Enchanted Forests to the Modern World* (1988), *Fairy Tale as Myth / Myth as Fairy Tale* (1994), *Happily ever after: Fairy Tales, Children, and the Culture Industry* (1997), *When Dreams Came True: Classical Fairy Tales and Their Tradition* (1999), *Sticks and Stones: The Troublesome Success of Children's Literature from Slovenly Peter to Harry Potter* (2001).

But there is also the fantastic *Oxford Companion to Fairy Tales* (2000) that Prof. Zipes edited as a reference book for everybody interested in the world of fairy tales. This volume is clearly one of the best resources for scholars and students of folk narratives. And I must also not forget the many beautiful anthologies that Prof. Zipes has published in his very own translations with explanatory notes, among them: *Don't Bet on the Prince: Contemporary Feminist Fairy Tales in North America and England* (1986), *The Complete Fairy Tales of the Brothers Grimm* (1987), *Beauties, Beasts, and Enchantment: Classic French Fairy Tales* (1989), *Fairy Tales and Fables from Weimar Days* (1989), *Spells of Enchantment: The Wondrous Fairy Tales of Western Culture* (1991), *Outspoken Princess and the Gentle Knight: A Treasury of Modern Fairy Tales* (1994), and *The Great Fairy Tale Tradition: From Straparola and Basile to the Brothers Grimm* (2001).

Prof. Zipes is, of course, also well known for his literary studies that are informed by a theoretical, political, and comparative approach. More than thirty years after its publication, his study on *The Great Refusal: Studies of the Romantic Hero in German and American Literature* (1970) remains a major contribution to the field of comparative literature, and his books on

Political Plays for Children: The Grips Theater of Berlin (1976), *Utopian Tales from Weimar* (1990), and *Struwelpeter: Fearful Stories and Vile Pictures to Instruct Good Little Folks* (1999) are clear indications of his interest in the ideological politics of culture.

Regarding his expertise in Holocaust and Jewish studies, let me also mention at least some of the significant book publications by this indefatigable scholar. There is first of all his translation and critical edition of *The Operated Jew: Two Tales of Anti-Semitism* (1991). Together with Anson Rabinbach he edited *Germans and Jews since the Holocaust: The Changing Situation in West Germany* (1986), and there is also the important essay volume on *Unlikely History: The Changing German-Jewish Symbiosis 1945-2000* (2002) that Prof. Zipes co-edited with Leslie Morris. A third and massive work is the *Yale Companion to Jewish Writing and Thought in German Culture, 1096-1996* (1997) that Jack Zipes edited with Sander L. Gilman who delivered the third annual Harry H. Kahn Memorial Lecture in 1992. There has also been a steady flow of scholarly articles penned by Jack Zipes, among them "The Holocaust and the Vicissitudes of Jewish Identity" (1980) and "The Negative German-Jewish Symbiosis" (1994).

Prof. Jack Zipes represents teaching and scholarship at their very best. His students have greatly benefitted from his vast knowledge and his commitment to comparative studies based on cultural studies that for him involve at least the American, English, French, German, Italian, and Yiddish languages and cultures. He is the perfect example for the necessity of studying foreign languages, and he has been a major cultural mediator in his role as a skilled translator. As a scholar he continues to have a lasting influence throughout the world, showing us that serious scholars should not hide in an ivory tower but rather step forth with work based on social insights and moral values.

Lecture

> "Jewish Child 1945"
>
> I do not have a name.
> I am a Jewish child.
> Don't know from where we came
> And where we'll be tomorrow,
>
> Many languages I've learned to speak
> And each in turn forgotten.
> For all we've had to bear
> Those languages are simply mute.
> Hermann Hakel

Ever since the publication of Theodor Adorno's essay "Cultural Criticism and Society" (1951) in which he provocatively declared "to write a poem after Auschwitz is barbaric," numerous writers and intellectuals, mainly in Germany, have sought to define, redefine, oppose, or support Adorno's thesis up to the present day. In fact, Adorno's statement has given rise to a virtual "Auschwitz industry" of intellectuals and artists who have produced poems, plays, novels and stories, not to mention all sorts of tracts and treatises concerned with the ethical, social, and aesthetic nature of poetry after Auschwitz.[1] Ironically, the obsession with Adorno's meaning has led to some obfuscation of postwar history. We have forgotten that numerous poets wrote remarkable poems right after 1945 in defiance of the barbarism of Auschwitz, and their poems, before and after Adorno, have constituted one of the more significant modes of writing with which Jews and non-Jews have sought to come to terms with the barbarity associated with Nazism. In particular, startling as it may seem, German Jews and Central European Jews continued writing poetry in German during and after Auschwitz to express not only their suffering and despair but their hope that they could contribute to the recuperation of a humanist tradition in Europe. Their unheard voices are voices that do not deserve to be obfuscated by Adorno's provocative remarks.

Yet, I do not want to blame Adorno for this obfuscation or to recuperate Jewish poetry after Auschwitz just for the sake of documenting once again that the Shoah was horrific, and that we should not forget what happened and who responded to it. That is, I do not want to discuss the nature of so-called Holocaust writing. Nor do I want to dismiss Adorno's remarks. Rather, I want to use Adorno's various essays about Auschwitz and poetry as the context to analyze three important anthologies of Jewish poetry in German published between 1959 and 1968: *Jüdisches Schicksal in deutschen Gedichten: Eine abschließende Anthologie* (1959) edited by Siegmund Kaznelson, *An den Wind geschrieben: Lyrik der Freiheit. Gedichte der Jahre 1933-1945* (1960) edited by Manfred Schlösser, *Welch Wort in die Kälte gerufen: Die Judenverfolgung des Dritten Reiches im deutschen Gedicht* (1968) edited by Heinz Seydel. I want to recuperate these neglected anthologies of poems and Adorno's essays about poetry after Auschwitz, that is, to recover and bring them back to life for the present, because we are in constant danger of falling prey to a barbaric fetishizing of the Holocaust and succumbing to the pressures of the culture industry. For the most part, Adorno's statement about the barbarity of poetry writing after Auschwitz has been lifted out of its own context, and it is only by returning to his initial essay, "Cultural Criticism and Society" and trying to grasp the categories he created in other essays for judging works of art in the post-Auschwitz period that we can recuperate neglected Jewish poetry in a meaningful way. First, Adorno needs some recuperating himself within a socio-historical context.

Like most German Jewish intellectuals of the Frankfurt School, Adorno, an assimilated Jew, whose mother was of Italian Catholic ancestry, never felt particularly drawn to Jewish concerns or compelled to write about anti-Semitism and the Jewish Question until the rise of Nazism in the 1930s. Forced to flee Germany in 1938 and shaken by the destruction of the humanist tradition, not only in Germany but throughout the world, Adorno turned his attention toward understanding what had gone wrong with the tradition of Enlightenment. Once he emigrated to New York, he never stopped writing about prejudice, totalitarianism, anti-Semitism, authoritarianism, and their negative effects on humanist culture. In the United States he collaborated with Max Horkheimer on the significant study, *Dialectic of the Enlightenment* (1944), which laid the basis for most of his future critical work. With the support of the American Jewish Committee, he participated in a project devoted to examining prejudice in the

United States. It eventually led to the publication of *The Authoritarian Personality* in 1950. By this time, however, Adorno had already returned to West Germany and was lecturing as a professor of philosophy and sociology at the Wolfgang-Goethe Universität in Frankfurt am Main. The major reasons for his going back to Germany were the rise of McCarthyism, the actions of the House Committee on un-American activities, and his deep concern about the negative impact of the culture industry in America. For Adorno, these were dangerous indices of a new kind of totalitarianism that was part of an administered society and resulted from the deformation of the Enlightenment. Germany was by no means a refuge for Adorno. But he believed he could be more effective in Germany, where his writings and lectures would have an impact on the younger generation. This is why the essay, "Cultural Criticism and Society," is so significant. Written in America during 1949, the year he returned to Germany, and published in 1951, this essay is a programmatic statement about his role as a critic and the role of criticism during barbaric times.

There are three basic questions that he poses in this essay. What is the role of the critic in the post-Auschwitz society? What has happened to culture? What are the conditions under which art is produced? Adorno begins his essay by demonstrating how the critic's function developed in bourgeois society from that of the reviewer who disseminated news about books and art into the twentieth-century professional critic, who believes himself to be omniscient and essentially affirms the *status quo.* Such a cultural critic believes that he or she is above society and possesses true knowledge of culture, but all this is self-deception. "The notion of free expression of opinion, indeed, that of intellectual freedom itself in bourgeois society, upon which cultural criticism is founded, has its own dialectic. For while the mind extricated itself from a theological-feudal tutelage, it has fallen increasingly under the anonymous sway of the *status quo.* This regimentation, the result of the progressive socialization of all human relations, did not simply confront the mind from without; it immigrated into its immanent consistency. It imposes itself as relentlessly on the autonomous mind as heteronomous orders were formerly imposed on the mind which was bound. Not only does the mind mould itself for the sake of its marketability, and thus reproduce the socially prevalent categories. Rather it grows to resemble ever more closely the *status quo* even where it subjectively refrains from making a commodity of itself. The network of the whole is drawn ever tighter, modelled after the act of exchange. It leaves the individual consciousness less and less room for evasion, preforms it more and more thoroughly, cuts it off *a priori* as it were from the possibility of differencing itself as all difference degenerates to a nuance in the monotony of supply."[2]

If the critic cannot separate himself/herself from the material conditions of society, then the critic must analyze art with the understanding that he/she is unfree and speak and write to negate this unfreedom. Otherwise, there will be no such thing as culture. "Culture is only true when implicitly critical, and the mind which forgets this revenges itself in the critics it breeds. Criticism is an indispensable element of culture which is itself contradictory: in all its untruth still as true as culture is untrue. Criticism is not unjust when it dissects -- this can be its greatest virtue -- but rather when it parries by not parrying" (22).

The critic's role is to deny that there is such a thing as culture per se, that is, culture is not absolute, eternal, and universal but is the outcome of social forces. Culture in a given society is constituted by the art and philosophy that distinguish themselves by holding forth the promise that humans can become free and independent. In this regard, in order for culture to be culture it cannot serve the vested interests of a particular group but must implicitly critique all forms of ideology, enslavement and manipulation. The quandary of culture is that socio-economic forces have brought about its degeneration into ideology so that culture in bourgeois society is intended to mask the way human beings are made into commodities and are bound to a socio-economic system that totally structures their lives to serve the dominant interests of the corporate business world. Under these conditions culture can thus be nothing but barbaric. Yet, bourgeois culture is not totally barbaric because it retains its original promise of freedom, and in withdrawing from itself, negating the existing state of affairs and the instrumentalization of the life-process, culture keeps alive the hope of freedom and resists contamination. The function of the cultural critic who refuses to be a cultural critic is therefore dialectical: he/she must recognize his/her complicity in consumer culture while at the same time confront society with its ideals that cannot be fulfilled under the existing socio-economic system. "The fact that theory becomes real force when it moves men is founded in the objectivity of the mind itself which, through the fulfillment of its ideological function must lose faith in ideology. Prompted by the incompatibility of ideology and existence, the mind, in displaying its blindness also displays its effort to free itself of ideology. Disenchanted the mind perceives naked existence in its nakedness and delivers it up to criticism. The mind either damns the material base, in accordance with the ever-questionable criterion of its 'pure principle', or it becomes aware of its own questionable position, by virtue of its incompatibility with the base. As a result of the social dynamic, culture becomes cultural criticism, which preserves the notion of culture while demolishing its present manifestations as mere commodities and means of brutalization. Such critical consciousness remains subservient to culture in so far as its concern with culture distracts from the true horrors" (28).

Adorno is insistent about this: cultural criticism must be replaced by dialectical criticism if culture is to be meaningful. "What distinguishes dialectical from cultural criticism is that it heightens cultural criticism until the notion of culture itself is negated, fulfilled and surmounted in one" (29). Adorno does not separate criticism from culture and society, but criticism must become self-reflective and aware of the ideological transformation of culture to serve dominant interest groups if there is going to be genuine culture. In this regard we all live in a world of appearances that veil the manner in which we work and are manipulated to serve particular interest groups. The task of the critic is not so much to expose the interest groups, "but rather to decipher the general social tendencies which are expressed in these phenomena and through which the most powerful interests realize themselves. Cultural criticism must become social physiogomy. The more the whole divests itself of all spontaneous elements, is socially mediated and filtered, is 'consciousness', the more it becomes 'culture'. In addition to being the means of subsistence, the material process of production finally unveils itself as that which it always was, from its origins in the exchange-relationship as the false consciousness which the two contracting parties have of each other: ideology" (30-31).

For Adorno, the totalizing nature of culture as ideology and the administered society as a mediating system that benefits particular powerful interest groups in control of the economy and public institutions constituted barbarism. Whenever he wrote about barbarism or the barbaric, Adorno was not simply referring to Nazism and the Shoah, but to all those social tendencies that perpetuated the appearance of culture, that is, untruth, deception, and empty thinking. Barbarism is the result of totalizing forces that seek to wipe out particularism and efface the distinct differences of individual subjects. Mechanically functioning categories and laws are established to maintain the untruth of truth and to govern our thinking and actions so that we do not recognize or realize how our world is socially constructed. It is by negating the legitimation of untruth and holding on to the negative position in dialectical thinking that Adorno saw a possibility of hope for culture against what had become civilized barbarity. But this hope was tempered by a healthy dose of skepticism.

Let us recall the closing words of his essay: "The more total society becomes, the greater the reification of the mind and the more paradoxical its effort to escape reification on its own. Even the most extreme consciousness of doom threatens to degenerate into idle chatter. Cultural criticism finds itself faced with the final stage of the dialectic of culture and barbarism. To write poetry after Auschwitz is barbaric. And this corrodes even the knowledge of why it has become impossible to write poetry today. Absolute reification, which presupposed intellectual progress as one of its elements, is now preparing to absorb the mind entirely. Critical intelligence cannot be equal to this challenge as long as it confines itself to self-satisfied contemplation" (34).

Whether one should write poetry after Auschwitz, as we can now see, was not the crucial question for Adorno in 1949. His essay, "Cultural Criticism and Society," was written to elaborate his role as critic for himself and like-minded thinkers, in contrast to the traditional cultural critic, in the West, in particular in Germany, at a time when culture itself had become civilized barbarism throughout the world. The dialectical principles of criticism that he outlines in this essay were also intended to encourage other critics to take this position, and moreover, they suggest aesthetic criteria by which one can distinguish between *reified poetry* that maintains the status quo and *authentic poetry* that exposes the brutalization and lies that Auschwitz represented. Auschwitz did not die with the end of Auschwitz, nor does Adorno postulate that Auschwitz is tied to one group, namely the Nazis or the Germans – something that we have sorrowfully been compelled to realize up to the present. In fact, by assuming that the barbarism of Auschwitz had stopped with the fall of Nazism would play into the hands of the culture industry and would lead to the fetishization of the Shoah as a commodity, something that has indeed happened since Adorno wrote his essay.[3]

To avoid this, Adorno insists that the truth content of the works produced by critics and artists alike must lead to the exposure of all the mediating elements that socialize us to disregard difference and particularity and to accept the totalizing images that pass for a reality that cannot or should not be changed. Such socialization for Adorno was barbaric in that it tended toward making disposable commodities out of people in the interest of ideology.

I do not believe that it would be an exaggeration to argue that the essay, "Cultural Criticism and Society," served as the basis for most of Adorno's critical works until his untimely death in 1969. Whenever he returned to the passage about "writing poetry after Auschwitz," -- and he did this in several essays -- it was not to determine whether one should or should not feel guilty about writing poetry or creating art after Auschwitz. Rather, as his last book, *Aesthetic Theory*, published posthumously in 1973, indicates, he sought to grasp what the authentic work of art was in a "half-barbaric society that is tending toward total barbarism."[4] One aspect of the authentic artwork is its refusal to comply with the commodification of art and its rejection of the edict that no more art can be made or that art is unnecessary. It is exactly in the nonnecessity of art that Adorno locates its necessity and authenticity. Adorno makes it eminently clear that authentic art is "an art that refuses to let itself be terrorized by positive ideology" (252) and forms the negative dialectics of culture. For Adorno, "culture checks barbarism, which is worse; it not only represses nature but conserves it through its repression; this resonates in the concept of culture, which originates in agriculture. Life has been perpetuated through culture, along with the idea of a decent life; its echo resounds in authentic artworks. Affirmation does not bestow a halo on the status quo; in

sympathy with what exists, it defends itself against death, the te-
los of all domination. Doubting this comes only at the price of
believing that death itself is hope" (252).

If culture is opposed to death, then poetry is not only possible after Auschwitz, but it is also crucial for the preservation of
humanism against barbarism. The question for Adorno was what
kind of poetry is crucial after Auschwitz, and here, too, he constantly wrote about this topic after his return to Germany. In his
incisive essay, "Talk on Poetry and Society," (1957) he sought to
outline some of the basic features of poetry that made it so vital
for the future development of a humanist culture. Adorno's basic
principle is that all individualistic poetry is by necessity social
because it is constituted by the general language of the poet's
times and is influenced by social developments. On the other
hand, the poem distinguishes itself from the general norms of society by spontaneously questioning these norms and expressing
the specific concerns of the individual through unique images.
"Its distance from mere existence becomes the measure of all
that is false and bad in existence. In protest against this the poem
gives expression to the dream of a world in which it would be
different. The idiosyncracy of the poetical spirit against the ex-
cessive power of things is a form of reaction against the reification of the world, the domination of commodities over human
beings that has been spreading since the beginnings of moder-
nity, ever since the industrial revolution evolved itself into the
ruling power of life."[5]

All this does not mean that we must read poetry by applying
sociological methods to grasp the social import of poetry. Nor
should poetry directly reflect the socio-political conditions in
which people live. Such direct reflection or representation would
only reproduce false images of society. It is the metaphorical capacity of poetry to transform experience into expressive forms
about the inexpressible that concerns Adorno, and he argues for
an immanent approach to poetry, just as he maintained that the
critic must recognize the immanence of his/her position in order
to assume a dialectical negative perspective. In other words, the
reader/critic must read from the words, images, metaphors of the
poem to grasp the individualistic opposition of the poet to the
social whole. It is through the immanent understanding of a
poem that one can appreciate the social import of the poem.

For Adorno, great poetry carries within itself a rupture. This rupture in and for itself is expressed by the individual poet's distancing himself or herself from society that has caused such alienation. The poem thus seeks to restore, as it were, harmony with nature by an intensification with the plight of the individual. "Only through humanization (*Vermenschlichung*) is nature to be given back the right once again that human domination of nature took away from it. Even lyrical (poetical) constellations in which no remainder of the conventional and objective existence, no crude materiality, no longer crept into them, the highest that our language knows, owe their dignity exactly to the power with which the I awakes the appearance of nature in them, withdrawing from alienation. Their pure subjectivity, that which seems unbreakable (seamless, *bruchlos*) and harmony in them, gives evidence of the opposite, of suffering from an existence that estranges the subject as well as love for it -- indeed, their harmony is actually nothing else than the merging voices of such suffering and such love" (80-81)

As we know, Adorno firmly believed that the advent of capitalism brought about a major crisis of individualism that was connected to the manner in which humans economically and socially organized themselves to exploit nature and thus exploited themselves. If nature itself was to be rescued from the reifying process of industrial society, it would mean that humans would have to abandon the quest to dominate nature. Paradoxically such an abandonment would lead to a re-humanization of the human being's own nature. In this regard, poetry as an individual manifestation of the possibility to live differently, that is, to live in harmony with nature was also anti-barbaric, and its ruptures with the barbaric tendencies of post-Auschwitz society were what made poetry crucial for the preservation of culture.

It is within the context of Adorno's understanding of poetry's role to preserve culture against barbaric tendencies that I now want to turn to the three anthologies: *Jüdisches Schicksal in deutschen Gedichten: Eine abschließende Anthologie* (1959) edited by Siegmund Kaznelson, *An den Wind geschrieben: Lyrik der Freiheit. Gedichte der Jahre 1933-1945* (1960) edited by Manfred Schlösser, *Welch Wort in die Kälte gerufen: Die Judenverfolgung des Dritten Reiches im deutschen Gedicht* (1968) edited by Heinz Seydel. Each one of these collections is a political and social intervention in the German discussion about poetry after Auschwitz, and implicit in the work of the editor, there is a response to Adorno's dictum "to write poetry after Auschwitz is barbaric." But as we have seen, Adorno was endeavoring to elaborate aesthetic and political categories for the necessity of writing poetry in barbaric times, and it is with his views in mind that I want to recuperate the significance of these anthologies.

Since it will be impossible to examine all the numerous poems and poets in the three collections, I want to discuss the significance of each collection and then analyze briefly how poets used their writing in different ways to counter and subvert the barbaric tendencies of their times. I do not intend to judge which poems are more worthy to be considered "great" or "genuine" poetry after Auschwitz in keeping with Adorno's notions. Much of the poetry published in these anthologies by Jewish survivors can be considered outpourings of the heart, emotional confrontations with their experiences that probe the human capacity to inflict torture on other humans, and passionate statements about the necessity to give birth to a different language and more humane society. They are simple, blunt, naked assertions. They are warnings and resolutions. My concern will be to select those poems by *neglected* Jewish writers who endeavor to express that the imaginable cannot be imagined and suggest that Auschwitz will always be with us and is in all of us. After all, Adorno's greatest contribution to our understanding of culture after Auschwitz was his realization that Auschwitz was by necessity in all of us and that all writing must reflect upon this and negate it at the same time. Otherwise, there would be no genuine culture. Only barbarism.

———

Siegmund Kaznelson completed the editing of *Jüdisches Schicksal in deutschen Gedichten: Eine abschließende Anthologie* in November of 1958 while living in Jerusalem. A Zionist from Poland, who had established the Jüdischer Verlag in Berlin in the 1920s and then emigrated to Palestine in 1937, he returned to Berlin in 1957 to re-establish the Jüdischer Verlag and died in 1959 after compiling this anthology. He purposely called the book a "concluding anthology" not only because "it concludes a

thousand-year historical period but also because poetry with
Jewish content in the German language will come to an end with
our generation or perhaps the next as far as anyone can judge.
So, this anthology is a warning, a legacy of the dead for the living, a legacy of the destroyed German Judaism for the survivors."[6] Fortunately, Jewish poetry in the German language has
not come to an end. His prophecy has not been fulfilled. Yet,
Kaznelson's compilation of poems about "Jewish fate" largely
by Jewish authors that date back to the Middle Ages is still valuable, for it is the only anthology of German-Jewish poems that
covers the period from the thirteenth century to 1946 and documents how closely Jewish writers were tied to the German cultural tradition.

Divided into eighteen sections such as "The Ancestors,"
"The Way and Mission of the Jew," "We and They," "Eternal
Wandering," "The Nobility of Suffering," "Presentiment of Disaster," "Exile," Martyrdom," and "Return," the collection often
tends to compartmentalize the poetry to demonstrate Jewish fateful history and its great artistic accomplishments. On the other
hand, it is one of the rare books that enables readers to gain a
sense of how Jews struggled with the German language, to appropriate it before their identities were appropriated. The loss of
self is striking in Rahel Levin's poem "Einsam" ("Lonely,"
1811, p.171):

> Each one
> Is lonely,
> Even
> Loves alone,
> And no one
> Can help the other.

Levin's poem is highly significant because it was one of the
first written by an assimilated Jew, who married a Christian and
was allegedly successful in integrating into German society of
the early nineteenth century. Yet, as her letters and memoirs
have revealed, she never overcame a sense of isolation and stig-
matization as Jew and as a woman. The pressure to assimilate,
the desire to be accepted and to know that one could never be
truly accepted for what she or he was is a theme that runs
through a great deal of the Jewish poetry in Kaznelson's volume.

There is a whole section in the anthology titled "'Judenschmerz': Abschied und Einsamkeit" ("Jewish Pain": Departure and Loneliness) that contains poems by Heinrich Heine, Peter Altenberg, Ludwig Fulda, Walter Calé, Arthur Schnitzler, J. J. David, Hedwig Lachmann, Richard Beer-Hoffmann, Erich Mühsam, Theodor Lessing, Alfred Wolfenstein, Albert Ehrenstein, and Gertrud Kolmar that reflect the estrangement that Jews felt in German and Austrian society and continued to feel after 1945. Perhaps the most poignant poem here is Mühsam's "Wer fragt nach mir?"("Who Will Ask about Me?" 188).

> "Who Will Ask about Me?"
> Who will ask about me when I'm dead?
> The gloomy day took away my youth.
>
> Evening came too soon. The rain poured.
> Happiness slipped away from me -- me the stranger.
>
> My poor heart has had enough suffering,
> Soon the night will come without stars.
>
> (Published in *Wüste – Krater – Wolken. Die Gedichte von Erich Mühsam*. Berlin: Paul Cassirer, 1914)

Mühsam, a Bohemian poet, who played an important role in the Bavarian Soviet Republic in 1918-19, spent the 1920s living from hand to mouth and writing provocative poetry. An antifascist, he was targeted by the Nazis when they came to power in 1933 and brutally murdered in Buchenwald in 1934. Kaznelson's anthology was one of the first postwar collections to honor Mühsam and others like Gertrud Kolmar and Gertrud Kantorowicz, who did not survive the Shoah.

But what about those who did? How did they use language to articulate their experiences? How did they want to use their words in light of the barbarism of the post-Auschwitz society?

Ilse Blumenthal-Weiss, who survived the camps, could not remain in Europe after 1945. She emigrated to New York, where she published numerous poems in German dedicated to recalling and overcoming the Holocaust. Her poem about her son, "Für Peter David Blumenthal" (Geboren 4. April 1921, Berlin; ermordet 23. Oktober 1941, Mauthausen) is indicative of much of her writing:

So I wander through a thousand martyrs' cells
and pluck a thousand pains from the walls.
And a thousand dreams that surround the night.
They arise from a thousand volumes of images:

In each corner your voice can still be heard.
In every gentle breeze your laughing still resounds.
And every beam of light that illuminates the room
Is like a reflection of your glistening eyes.
Are you dead? -- Dead. I must slowly learn this
That one can so completely destroy the light.

I must learn when they say: *Murder!*
That this word, that this one word
Means you, you, young child's blood,
You: Jubilation! Cheering! Youth! High Spirits! --
God has taken. Once God had given.
I must learn to live without you.

(Published in *Mahnmal. Gedichte aus dem KZ*, edited by
the Akademie der Wissenschaften und der Literatur,
Mainz. Hamburg: Christian Wegner, 1957)

Throughout her poetry, Blumenthal-Weiss seeks to grasp what
words such as murder really mean, and what it means to live after murder, recalling the hopes that decent people had. Some of
her poems simply want to document the extinction of anonymous individuals to dignify their anonymity. Thus in a poem
such as "Prisoners" ("Häftlinge," 358), she concludes:

I know no name and know no trace.
A Jew was killed. Just a Jew.
With my tears as a death offering
I carry the Jewish corpse to its grave.

(Published in *Mahnmal*, 1957)

An individual has been obliterated, and it is against such oblit-
eration and contemporary oblivion of the causes and nature of
human destruction that Blumenthal-Weiss writes. The meters
and rhyme schemes of her poems are traditional. Unlike Paul
Celan, Nelly Sachs, and Hilde Domin, she is not innovative in
her use of language. Nevertheless, the simple candor of her verse

is powerful as she describes in such poems as "Transport-Ankunft," "Transport-Abgang," and "Selektion" how the systematic annihilation contrived by the Nazis functioned to deaden the aspirations of unique individuals who are rounded up like animals and become nameless.

Although Mascha Kaléko did not suffer in the camps the way Ilse Blumenthal-Weiss did, her poetry in this anthology reveals how she, too, sought to employ the German language in a terse simple manner to make clear what Auschwitz meant for her. Born 1907 in Schidlow, which is today Chrzanow, Poland, Kaléko's father was Russian, and her mother, Austrian. During World War I the family moved to Marburg, but she spent her school and university years in Berlin, where she mixed in Bohemian circles connected to the Romanisches Café. During the 1920s she began writing poetry and prose for the *Vossische Zeitung* and *Berliner Tageblatt*. Her first major anthology of poems, *Lyrisches Stenogrammheft* (1933) was a bestseller and simultaneously burned by the Nazis. Despite difficulties, she kept publishing poetry in Germany until her emigration to New York with her husband, Chemjo Vinaver, a composer, in 1938. In 1945, she published an important collection of poems entitled *Verse für Zeitgenossen* and returned to Germany for the first time in 1956. By 1966, she moved to Israel and continued writing poetry in German. She made numerous trips to Europe to do readings and died 1975 in Zurich on her way back from a reading in Berlin to her home in Jerusalem.

Her poems in this anthology such as "Emigranten-Monolog" ("The Monologue of an Emigrant"), "Einmal möcht' ich dort noch gehen. . . ," ("One time I Would Still Like to Go There. . ."), and "Einem kleinen Emigranten," ("To a Little Emigrant") focus on her experiences in exile and the feeling of isolation and paralysis that will never leave her. In "Unter fremdem Dach" ("Beneath a Strange Roof"), she writes:

Nights I hear the rain
Beneath a strange roof.
Rain . . . Rain . . .
How you keep me awake
Beneath a strange roof.

The rain roared that way
In that year . . .
Through singing birch trees
In dripping wet hair,
In my homeland
Fountains.

Now I no longer hear it roar
From the spring and the brook.
Now I always hear it roar
From tears.

Rain . . . Rain . . .
Beneath a strange roof
I've laid too long,
Too long have I laid.

(Published in *Verse für Zeitgenossen*. Hamburg: Rowohlt, 1958)

There is a sense of despair and longing in Kaléko's poems.
Exile cannot provide a new sense of home, and it appears that
she will be compelled to wander forever. This is also the case in
Berthold Viertel's poetry. Born 1885 in Vienna, Viertel attended
the University of Vienna and studied history and philosophy. As
a student he began publishing poetry and art reviews in leading
literary journals in Austria and Germany such as *Simplicissimus,
Die Schaubühne*, and *Die Fackel*. During this time he developed
a close relationship with Karl Kraus, the imposing literary critic
and editor of *Die Fackel*. In 1911, he became one of the founders
of the Wiener Volksbühne and began his prominent career as a
theater director working in Dresden, Berlin, and Düsseldorf. In
1923 he founded the experimental ensemble "Die Truppe," and
in 1928 he traveled to Hollywood, where he spent four years di-
recting films. After spending one year in Germany, he emigrated
to Paris but worked for the most part in London from 1933-39.
Then he emigrated to New York and worked as a film director in
Hollywood, where he adapted Bertolt Brecht's *Furcht und Elend
des Dritten Reichs* (Fear and Misery of the Third Reich) for the
screen. Throughout his exile Viertel continued to write poetry
and became one of the founders of the Aurora Publishing House
in New York that printed books by exile authors in the German

language. In 1948 he returned to Vienna and was active in theaters in Vienna, Zurich, Berlin, and Salzburg until his death in 1953. Though he seemed to make adjustments to different societies throughout his life, his poetry reveals a deep discontent with the way the world "adjusted" itself to what occurred during and after the Holocaust. For instance, "Scribbling on the Back of a Passport" ("Gekritzel auf der Rückseite eines Reisepasses") is a cynical view of exile.

> One is not born with a passport.
> One learns a language as a child.
> In the end the meaning of the words
> that were useful were lost.

> What home meant now means hell
> From which one escaped in the nick of time.
> And new borders, new tolls,
> But seldom is there a little shame.

> There are the places and the times.
> Once one was young, now one becomes old.
> Yet one must still pay for
> the trip and the stay.

> That's the way people are and the empires.
> One emigrates and immigrates.
> But everywhere it is the same.
> The brains, made of wax, the hearts, of stone.

> (Published in *Dichtungen und Dokumente*. Munich: Kösel, 1956)

Whereas Kaznelson's anthology was composed with the belief that poetry dealing with Jewish culture and the destiny of Jews would soon end, and therefore, it was important to mark the contribution that Jews made to German culture, Schlösser's collection of poems, *An den Wind geschrieben: Lyrik der Freiheit. Gedichte der Jahre 1933-1945*, was done with the hope that a certain humanitarian tradition might be continued. The book begins with a moving quotation by Paul Celan:

"And there was a time when one heard a song resound in the wind in Germany like it was never sung before. A chorale made of a thousand voices that the wind carried on its back through the land, invisible, intangible, a consolation to some, a terror to the rulers of power. The wind collected the songs of freedom from the prisons and cellars, from the hidden rooms and from all the foreign places. It was the confidante of all the suffering people and did not sense that the days could come in which a small sound shift would ruin its mission. Whoever raised his voice for freedom and human rights wrote to the wind and on the day when freedom came, one soon forgot. Time passed. The words were written in the wind."[7]

(Published in *Der Tod ist ein Meister aus Deutschland*)

Schlösser's anthology wants to keep alive the poems that were written to the wind, and the very purpose of the Agora Publishing House, as stated at the end of the book, was to make neglected works of the past available for younger generations so that there could be a critical confrontation with the legacy of the humanist tradition in need of rejuvenation. There are twelve sections in this collection: Kassandra-Mars, Verbannung-Aufbruch, Fremde-Verfremdung, Erkennen-Verzweiflung, Verfolgung-Haft, Weltherbst-Fluch, Hiob-Ahasver, Grabschrift-Requiem, Gedenken-Zeit, Exil-Tote Heimat, Trost-Tröstung, Rückkunft-Wende. Given the fact that almost all the poems originated during the Nazi period, there is a tension throughout the book that adds intensity to the poems themselves. Written by German and Jewish poets in defiance of the barbarity of Nazism and to articulate their personal experiences, these poems appear together in 1960 as historical markers of the past that are to provide readers with modes of thinking and feeling that will make Auschwitz impossible in the future. In this regard their conception during the time of barbarism appears to enable them to suggest possibilities for creating poetry in post-Auschwitz times. Their selection for the anthology is predicated on such a viewpoint put forth by the editor.

Since the collection is large and it would be difficult to do justice to many of the fine poems, I want once more to single out several endeavors by Jewish poets to cope with the problems of writing in German to indicate how their poems are in some way in keeping with Adorno's own endeavors to work through what it means to create poetry part of and critical of Auschwitz.

Here I want to begin with Martha Hoffmann, who was born 1905 in Vienna. After studying in Austria and Germany, she received a doctorate in Heidelberg and became a teacher, but was forced to flee Austria in 1938. In her poem "Robbed Language" ("Geraubte Sprache," 1941), she writes,

Oh, if I were like a cloud, like fog and haze,
so mute, since the evening's blaze,
I would not have to mold, robbed of language,
my art, the only one, while alive.

(Published in *Wandelsterne*. Vienna: Jupiter-Verlag, 1954)

The devastation caused by the loss of language is also poignant in two of Hans Sahl's poems. Born in Dresden in 1902, he became a film and theater critic in Berlin during the 1920s. After fleeing to France in 1933, he was interned in a concentration camp in 1939/40 in the South of France. Fortunately, he managed to gain his release and emigrate to the United States. In 1943 he wrote "Soon Oblivion Will Envelop Me" ("Bald hüllt Vergessenheit mich ein"):

I have not spoken a German word for a long time.
I go silently through the foreign land.
Only crumbs of the language that I find
spread about in my pockets remain.
Muted are they, the maternal sounds,
That I read astonishingly from her lips,
milk, tree and brook, the cats that meowed,
Moon and stars, the one times one of the night.

The woods have never smelled so foreign.
No fairy tale calls me, no good fairy.
I have not spoken a German word for a long time.
Soon oblivion will envelop me like snow.

(Manuscript, first published in the present collection.)

There is a nostalgia for the German language in many poems by
Hoffmann, Jacob Haringer, and others. It is as though the Jewish
poets, who often felt secure in their German or Austrian identity,
cannot believe that things cannot be as they were, and they are
traumatized, compelled to rethink their connection to the German language and culture. On the other hand, there are those poets like Heinz Politzer and Berthold Viertel, who insist that this
language is theirs for good, and they stake out a claim in preserv-
ing the German language from being besmirched. Politzer, who
emigrated to the States and became a noted Kafka scholar, wrote
a poem "To the German Language" ("Auf die deutsche Sprache," 1943) which closes with the following lines:

> Yet now whorish, perverted by hate
> And completely orphaned among heathens, --
> When will you once again be transfigured,
> Oh language, in your spirit?

> But I shall hold your tiny light
> With my hand in careful attention.
> Like you, fading and banned,
> I shall go with you to the last judgment.

> (Published in *Die gläserne Kathedrale*. Vienna: Berg-
> land, 1959)

In a somewhat different vein and yet similar, Berthold Viertel
wrote "On Refusing to Speak German" ("Der Nicht mehr
Deutsch spricht,"):

> You say the German language is taboo,
> Because of our rage and shame.
> But how speak then to your dead,
> None of whom escaped with you?

> To the friends who suffered for you,
> Who were captured instead of you,
> How beg their forgiveness
> If their words are no longer in you?

And however pure your English locution,
Those bastards wouldn't care:
You could swallow your original tongue,
They'd still concoct a final solution.

The spoiled child, sure he's right,
Who sulks, and punishes his mother
By refusing to eat, this is that:
Infantile; a tantrum, spite.

(Translated by C. K. Williams, first published in *Der Lebenslauf*. New York: Auora, 1946)

For most of the poets writing during the period 1933-1945, the question of language and its corruption by the Nazis was acute. Whether they addressed it directly, this question was perhaps the propelling motif implicit in most of their writing: how to keep humanist tradition alive through the German language despite the barbarity of the Nazis? For Jews the question was even more specific: should one or could one write in the language of one's murderers? This question shifts somewhat in the post-Auschwitz period, and I now want to turn to some of the poems in the anthology edited by Heinz Seydel to explore the attitudes of Jewish poets to the German language and their experiences before and after Auschwitz.

Welch Wort in die Kälte gerufen: Die Judenverfolgung des Dritten Reiches im deutschen Gedicht is a curious and rare book. Published 1968 by the Verlag der Nation in the former German Democratic Republic, the book is the only collection of verse that addressed Jewish persecution and was published in East Germany. Like most books in the former GDR, it did not have a large printing and quickly went out of print. Moreover, as the introduction makes clear, the book was intended politically to enlighten young readers in the German Democratic Republic so that Nazism would not reoccur, to intervene in discussions in West Germany at a time when Jewish cemeteries were being destroyed and former SS leaders were allegedly playing a leading role in the West German economy, and finally to demonstrate solidarity between communists and Jews, who allegedly suffered the same fates during the Nazi period. Obviously, the moralistic pathos of the introduction served to conceal the mistreatment of Jews in East Germany after 1945 and the political machinations of the East German government. Nevertheless, the anthology speaks for itself, that is, the individual poems speak for themselves and often contradict and expose the ideological blabber of the introduction.

Like the other collections, this one, too, is neatly divided into themes such as diaspora, presentiment, exile, pogroms, deportation, ghetto, concentration camp, children, death thoughts, and aftermath. The poems are written by German and Jewish poets and stem from the nineteenth century to 1968. Here I want to create a montage of stanzas from several poems that illustrate how fragile and yet how necessary poetry is after Auschwitz. This montage is composed of poems by lesser-known Jewish poets in Germany and Austria whose lines recall personal experiences that may be difficult for us to imagine, and yet, the poets want us to imagine what it might have been like for us, and why it should not be similar for us. As poems they open up critical questions about the nature of culture, and as a montage, I hope that the images will enable you to see how the poems are very much connected to Adorno's own endeavors to shape an anti-barbaric culture in the postwar period.

> I eat and drink. I sigh in the dream.
> I drag myself along through the groaning land.
> Steps fade away in the endless space. --
> I eat and drink. I sigh in the dream.
> I grasp into the emptiness with my helpless hand.

> (Ilse Blumenthal-Weiß, "Rückkehr aus dem KZ" in *Mahnmal*. Hamburg: Christian Wegner, 1958)

> We travel through Germany, my child.
> And it is night.
> The dead accuse in the wind --
> and nobody has wakened up . . .

> ("Schlaflied für Daniel," Siegfried Einstein in *Das Wolkenschiff*. Zurich, Verlag Beer & Co., 1950)

My house stands on top of the mountain
so that I see it
Throbbing pulses are its stairs
that I do not climb
Thirsty eyes are its windows
that I do not open
When the wind carries flakes
I feel that I am freezing
When the wind carries sparks
I feel that I am burning
easy to see from the lake
sick a scraggy flag
in my house on the mountain
where I am not

("Heimweh," Erich Fried in *Gedichte*. Hamburg: Claassen, 1958)

I'm not dead -- they did not kill me,
I can still speak -- but to whom?
I hear a stranger saying words --
Am I the stranger --? Am I speaking to him?

("Selbstgespräch," Kurt Frankenschwerth in *Seid ihr wach?* Munich: Kurt Desch, 1947)

It will not be enough to say to you, "From today on
    you'll be like your good old self again."
I can see it in you: you dream about your craft.
The handle on the knife will make you remember.
The solitary stroller will kindle your desire.
The women will be horrified when you hold their
children up high,
and the men will stop speaking when they see you.
Your craft is still in you, I can see it in you.
Hide yourself.

("Heimkehrender Mörder spricht zu seiner Hand,"
Günther Anders, first published in this anthology)

The day is held still
as with threads.
Roses still glow
beyond time, unbent.

And you are obliterated
and gone, my dear ones?
Who still says, one lives,
another disappeared?

Roses, appearing,
memory still glowing . . .
And the day is held still
as with threads.

("Gedenken," Eduard Saenger in *Die fremden Jahre*
Heidelberg: Lambert Schneider, 1959)

In later times one will read about us.
I never wanted to arouse the sympathy
of school children in later times.
Never in this way
to be in a schoolbook.

We, condemned
to know
and not to act.

Our dust
will never more become earth.

("Von uns," Hilde Domin in *Hier*. Frankfurt am Main:
Fischer, 1964)

Of course, the Jewish poets in the anthologies edited by
Kaznelson, Schlösser, and Seydel never wanted and probably
never thought that they would appear in books that sought to
make a statement about poetry after Auschwitz. They wrote and
published separately because they could not tolerate not being silent about what they had experienced in a civilization that was
demeaning the worth of the individual human being. To the extent that they mastered German words, forged and shaped them
into images that articulated feelings commensurable with their

experiences, their poems are effective. The very contention with the German language, that is, the manner in which the poets contended with the German language to deflate the ideological contamination of Nazism and the post-war propaganda of the East and the West determines the substance of the poetry. By no means were the Jewish poets hoping to "purify" the German language once again. Rather they embraced it and embodied the language with extraordinary metaphors and meters so that their voices could be heard above and against the hypocrisy of politicians and people eager to get on with their lives and function in keeping with the economic miracle in both Germany and Austria.

That the voices in these anthologies went largely unheard is due to many different factors in the period 1945 to 1968 ranging from the complex issue of shame and the inability to mourn manifested by many Germans and Austrians and the development of a culture industry in Germany and Austria that has minimized the effect of poems that expose the barbaric nature of the industry. Nevertheless, these anthologies did play a role in the formation of a German-Jewish dialogue and set the ground work for various kinds of writing that showed the necessity for poetry after Auschwitz. I have focused on the Jewish voices in the anthologies, but the editors, two of whom are not Jewish, also published poems by non-Jewish German and Austrian poets who wrote about similar themes addressed by the Jewish poets and wrote to negate those forms of culture that fostered barbarism. There is much to be said about this German-Jewish collaboration that goes beyond the negative German-Jewish symbiosis. But the poetry itself speaks about it and speaks for itself. It is the poetry that Adorno saw as necessary to bring about a redemption of culture.

Notes:

[1] For the best overview of this "industry," see Petra Kieddaisch, ed. *Lyrik nach Auschwitz? Adorno und die Dichter* (Stuttgart: Reclam, 1995). It contains Adorno's key essays and numerous responses by German poets and writers.

[2] Theodor W. Adorno, *Prisms*, trans. Samuel and Shierry Weber (Cambridge: MIT Press, 1981): 20-21. All future page references in the essay are taken from this text.

[3]Cf. Peter Novick, *The Holocaust in American Life* (Boston: Houghton Mifflin, 1999); Time Cole, *Selling the Holocaust: From Auschwitz to Schindler* (New York: Routledge, 1999); and Norman Finkelstein, *The Holocaust Industry. Reflections on the Exploitation of Jewish Suffering* (London: Verso, 2000).
[4]Theodor W. Adorno, *Aesthetic Theory*, trans. Robert Hullot-Kentor (Minneapolis: University of Minnesota Press, 1997): 251. All future page references in the essay are taken from this text.
[5]Theodor W. Adorno, "Rede über Lyrik und Gesellschaft" in *Noten zur Literatur* (Frankfurt am Main: Suhrkamp, 1958): 78. My translation. All future page references in the essay are taken from this text.
[6]Siegmund Kaznelson, *Jüdisches Schicksal in deutschen Gedichten: Eine abschließende Anthologie* (Berlin: Jüdischer Verlag, 1959): 14.
[7]In Manfred Schlösser, ed., *An den Wind geschrieben: Lyrik der Freiheit. Gedichte der Jahre 1933-1945* (Darmstadt: Agora, 1960): 1. All future references in the essay are taken from this book.

Bibliography

Adorno, Theodor W. "Kulturkritik und Gesellschaft," *Kulturkritik und Gesellschaft I: Prismen. Ohne Leitbild.* Frankfurt am Main: Suhrkamp, 1977: 11-30.
_____. *Prisms.* Trans. Samuel and Shierry Weber. Cambridge: MIT Press, 1981.
_____. "Rede über Lyrik und Gesellschaft," *Noten zur Literatur I.* Frankfurt am Main: Suhrkamp, 1958: 73-104.
_____. "Engagement," *Noten zur Literatur III.* Frankfurt am Main: Suhrkamp, 1965: 109-35;
_____. "Meditationen zur Metaphysik," *Negative Dialektik.* Frankfurt am Main: Suhrkamp, 1980: 354-61.
_____. *Ästhetische Theorie.* Ed. Gretel Adorno and Rolf Tiedemann. Frankfurt am Main: Suhrkamp, 1973.
_____. *Aesthetic Theory.* Ed. and trans. Robert Hullot-Kentor. Minneapolis: University of Minnesota Press, 1997.
Bernstein, Michael André. *Foregone Conclusions: Against Apocalyptic History.* Berkeley: University of California Press, 1994.
Grass, Günter. *Schreiben nach Auschwitz: Frankfurter Poetik-Vorlesung.* Frankfurt am Main: Luchterhand, 1990.
Heller, Agnes. "Die Weltuhr stand still. Schreiben nach Auschwitz? Schweigen über Auschwitz? Philosophische Betrachtungen eines Tabus." *Die Zeit* 19 (1993): 61 f.
Hessing, Jakob. "Gedichte nach Auschwitz." *Merkur* 46 (1992): 980-992.
Hohendahl, Peter. *Prismatic Thought: Theodor W. Adorno.* Lincoln: University of Nebraska Press, 1995.
Kaiser, Gerhard R., ed. *Poesie der Apokalypse.* Würzburg: Königshausen & Neumann, 1991.

Kaznelson, Siegmund, ed. *Jüdisches Schicksal in deutschen Gedichten: Eine abschließende Anthologie*. Berlin: Jüdischer Verlag, 1959.

Kiedaisch, Petra, ed. *Lyrik nach Auschwitz? Adorno und die Dichter*. Stuttgart: Reclam, 1995.

Köppen, Manuel, ed. *Kunst und Literatur nach Auschwitz*. Berlin: Erich Schmidt, 1993.

Laermann, Klaus. "Die Stimme bleibt. Theodor W, Adornos Dictum – Überlegungen zu einem Darstellungsverbot." *Die Zeit* 14 (March 27, 1992): 69.

Lamping, Dieter, ed. *Dein aschenes Haar Sulamith: Dichtung über den Holocaust*. Munich: Piper, 1992.

Lorenz, Otto. "Gedichte nach Auschwitz oder: Die Perspektive der Opfer" in *Bestandsaufnahme Gegenwartsliteratur*. Sonderband *text + kritik* (1988): 35-54.

Lüdke, Martin. "Zu reden wäre von der Echternacher Springprozession, Adorno und der Literatur nach Auschwitz" in *Vom Kahlschlag zum movens: über das langsame Auftauchen experimenteller Schreibweisen in der westdeutschen Literatur der 50er Jahre*, ed. Jörg Drews. Munich: text +kritik, 1980): 127 ff.

Meiners, R. K. "Mourning for Our Selves and for Poetry: The Lyric after Auschwitz." *The Centennial Review* 35 (1991): 545-590.

Nolte, Andreas. *"Mir ist zuweilen so als ob das Herz in mir zerbrach." Leben und Werk Mascha Kalékos im Spiegel ihrer sprichwörtlichen Dichtung*. Bern: Peter Lang, 2003.

Schlösser, Manfred, ed. *An den Wind geschrieben: Lyrik der Freiheit. Gedichte der Jahre 1933-1945*. Darmstadt: Agora, 1960.

Seydel, Heinz, ed. *Welch Wort in die Kälte gerufen: Die Judenverfolgung des Dritten Reiches im deutschen Gedicht*. Berlin: Verlag der Nation, 1968.

Young, James E. *Writing and Rewriting the Holocaust: Narrative and the Consequences of Interpretation*. Bloomington: University of Indiana Press, 1988.